WORLD BOOK'S

Celebrations and Rituals Around the World

World Book, Inc.
a Scott Fetzer Company
Chicago

This edition published in the United States of America by World Book, Inc., Chicago. WORLD BOOK and the GLOBE DEVICE are registered trademarks or trademarks of World Book, Inc.

World Book, Inc.
233 North Michigan Avenue
Chicago, IL 60601 U.S.A.

For information about other World Book publications, visit our Web site http://www.worldbook.com, or call 1-800-WORLDBK (967-5325).
For information about sales to schools and libraries, call: 1-800-975-3250 (United States); 1-800-837-5365 (Canada).

Library of Congress Cataloging-in-Publication Data
Religious celebrations.
p. cm. – (World Book's celebrations and rituals around the world)
Includes index.
Summary: Relates the ancient roots of various religious celebrations and describes how such occasions are observed in different countries and by different cultures around the world. Includes a recipe and activity.
ISBN 0-7166-5015-0
1. Fasts and feasts—Juvenile literature. 2. Festivals—Juvenile literature. [1. Fasts and feasts. 2. Festivals.] I. World Book, Inc. II. Series.
BV43 .R45 2003
291.3'6 21 2003041073

McRae Books:
Publishers: Anne McRae and Marco Nardi
Series Editor: Loredana Agosta
Graphic Design: Marco Nardi
Layout: Sebastiano Ranchetti
Picture Research: Helen Farrell, Claire Moore
Art Consultant: Andrea Ricciardi di Gaudesi
Cutouts: Filippo delle Monache, Alman Graphic Design
Text: Rupert Matthews, Cath Senker

Illustrations: Studio Stalio (Alessandro Cantucci, Fabiano Fabbrucci, Andrea Morandi, Ivan Stalio), Paola Ravaglia, Paula Holguin, Andrea Ricciardi di Gaudesi, Ferruccio Cucchiarini, Sabrina Marconi, MM (Manuela Cappon), Alessandro Menchi

Color Separations: Litocolor, Florence (Italy)

World Book:
Editorial: Maureen Liebenson, Sharon Nowakowski, Shawn Brennan
Research: Paul Kobasa, Cheryl Graham, Madolynn Cronk
Text Processing: Curley Hunter, Gwendolyn Johnson
Proofreading: Anne Dillon
Indexing: David Pofelski

Acknowledgments
The Publishers would like to thank the following photographers and picture libraries for the photos used in this book.
t=top; tl=top left; tc=top center; tr=top right; c=center; cl=center left; cr=center right; b= bottom; bl=bottom left; bc=bottom center; br=bottom right
AFP: 19tr; A.S.A.P Picture Library: 25cl, 30c, 31tr, 31cl; Corbis/Contrasto: 15tr, 23br; Dinodia: 19br; Marco Lanza: 20br, 34br; Lonely Planet Images: Marie Cambon 11tr, Adina Tovy Amsel 12cl, Christine Niven 17tr, Nick Ray 17cl, Greg Elms 22cl, Brenda Turnnidge 22br, Richard I'Anson 39br, Frances Linzee Gordon 40cr, Patrick Horton 43tr, Peter Ptschelinzew 43br; Bernadette Heath 37br; The Image Works: 11br, 12bl, 15tl, 17b, 18br, 21tr, 25br, 26tr, 27cl, 28cl, 29tr, 34tr, 34cl, 38bl, 39tr, 41tr, 41bl, 43cl

In the same series:
Birth and Growing Up Celebrations
End-of-Life Rituals
Everyday Celebrations and Rituals
Harvest Celebrations
Marriage Celebrations
National Celebrations
New Year's Celebrations
Spring Celebrations
Winter Celebrations
Cumulative Glossary and Index

Printed and bound in Hong Kong by C&C Offset
1 2 3 4 5 6 7 8 10 09 08 07 06 05 04 03

WORLD BOOK'S

CELEBRATIONS AND RITUALS AROUND THE WORLD

RELIGIOUS CELEBRATIONS

Religious Celebrations

Table of Contents

Ancient Celebrations

The Far East

South and Central Asia

The Middle East

Europe and the Americas

Africa

Australasia and Oceania

Glossary

Index

Introduction

The belief in supernatural spirits or gods is shared by many people all over the world. Followers of some religions, such as Judaism, Christianity, and Islam, believe in one supreme God. Followers of other religions, such as those native to China and Japan, worship spirits and many gods or deities. Buddhists, on the other hand, do not believe in a supreme being, but follow the teachings of Buddha, a spiritual teacher. For many, God is invisible and prophets communicate God's will. Prophets are individuals who are divinely inspired to reveal or interpret God's message. A prophet is also an individual who is considered a spiritual leader of a religious group, giving followers moral values and spiritual guidance. There are many religious feast days that commemorate prophets and religious leaders and the special events in their lives. Among these occasions are birthdays of special individuals, such as Christmas, when Christians celebrate the birth of Jesus Christ. These feast days can be solemn days set aside for prayer or occasions for celebration and merrymaking. Deities and spirits are also given special veneration on special occasions. Followers of the native religions of China and Japan have many local celebrations to honor the spirits and deities. Hindus worldwide also celebrate their deities with offerings, dance, and song on special feast days.

***Traditional Indian dances** based on stories from myth and sacred texts are performed during many Hindu religious feast days.*

Buddhists in Sri Lanka, above left, *parade through the streets with decorated elephants and a replica of the sacred tooth of Buddha.*

BIRTHDAYS OF RELIGIOUS LEADERS AND PROPHETS

Full Moon in Spring
Buddha (Indian prince Siddhartha Gautama, who founded Buddhism)

May
Tam Kung (man-god worshiped in Macao)

July
Haile Selassie (former Ethiopian emperor revered by Rastafarians)

August/September
Krishna (physical form of Hindu deity Vishnu)
Ganesa (elephant-headed god worshiped by Hindus)

September
Confucius (Chinese founder of Confucianism)

October
The Báb (Bahá'í prophet born in Persia)

October/November
Guru Nanak (Indian founder of Sikhism)

December
Jesus Christ

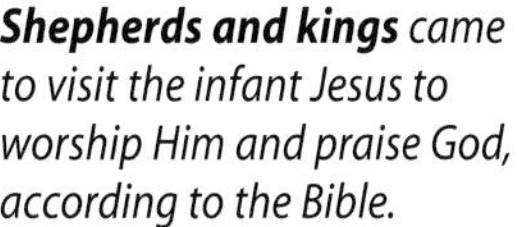

***Shepherds and kings** came to visit the infant Jesus to worship Him and praise God, according to the Bible.*

Ancient Gods and Goddesses

The peoples of the ancient world worshiped a variety of different gods and goddesses. Some people worshiped many different gods at the same time; some had a favorite deity. The gods and goddesses were believed to take an interest in their own special parts of the natural and human world. There were gods of harvest and war, goddesses of love and jealousy, and there were strange and terrifying gods of death and destruction. Sometimes the people of one nation would begin to worship a god revered in another country, or a god could lose followers and in time no longer be worshiped.

The god Amon-Re *was a combination of the ram-headed god Amon and the sun god Ra, who traveled in a boat. He appears in different human forms, sometimes with a ram head and sometimes without.*

During the festival of Amon-Re, a statue of the god was placed in a boat-shaped shrine, right, *and pulled through the city of Thebes by priests.*

Athena was one of many goddesses worshiped by the Greeks, left. *She was the patron of wisdom and of craftspeople. She was the special goddess of the city of Athens and was thought to protect the city with her sacred shield. The temple of Athena in Athens contained a huge statue of the goddess made of ivory and gold.*

Egyptian Feast Days

The Egyptians believed in many hundreds of different gods, some of which were alternative versions of a more important god. Many gods or goddesses were thought to protect a single village or town and were worshiped only in that place. Each god had its festival when the statue of the god was placed in a boat or cart and pulled around the city to be adored by the people.

The Panthenaic Festival was held in Athens every four years to honor Athena. *During the festival there were athletic races, rowing competitions, musical contests, and dances. The festival ended with a grand procession of the citizens of Athens to the Parthenon, a temple on the Acropolis built to honor Athena.*

Festivals in Ancient Greece

The ancient Greeks honored their gods by holding festivals and celebrations. Some of these were held each year, but the most important were held every four years. The Olympic Festival was celebrated at Olympia in honor of the great god Zeus. The festival included athletic games as well as religious rituals. The Delphic Festival was composed of theater performances and singing. The great festival held at Eleusis was dedicated to the earth goddess Demeter, but what happened was a secret that nobody was allowed to discuss or write down. The Festival was called the Eleusinian Mysteries.

Making Sacrifices to the Roman Gods

The Romans believed that they had to carry out rituals and sacrifices to honor the gods, or the gods would become angry and destroy the crops or bring bad luck. Farm animals were often sacrificed and their bones, fat, and intestines burned on an altar as food for the gods. The meat of the animal was then eaten by the worshipers during a ritual feast. The priests were men or women from the noble families of Rome, who were trained to perform the sacrifices and rituals exactly as the gods liked them to be done.

A Roman priest lights a fire on the altar *before sacrificing a pig, a sheep, and an ox to a god.*

Epona, the Celtic Horse Goddess

The Celts were a warlike people divided into many different tribes across western Europe. Several tribes had their own gods, but one goddess was worshiped by all Celts. This was Epona, the goddess of horses. She is usually shown leading one or two horses.

Ancient Celts worshiped Epona, *the goddess of horses,* left.

Aztec Human Sacrifice

The Aztec people of Central America, whose empire flourished during the A.D. 1400's and early 1500's, worshiped many gods and goddesses. For the Aztecs, the sun was the source of life and Huitzilopochtli, the sun and war god, was their patron god. The Aztecs built the Great Temple at their capital city of Tenochtitlan in honor of Huitzilopochtli. Thousands of humans were sacrificed to Huitzilopochtli each year at the temple to maintain order in the world and to ensure that the sun rose each day. During the sacrificial rite, male captives or slaves had to climb to the top of the temple where a priest would then cut out their hearts. The hearts were then placed in a stone bowl and burned.

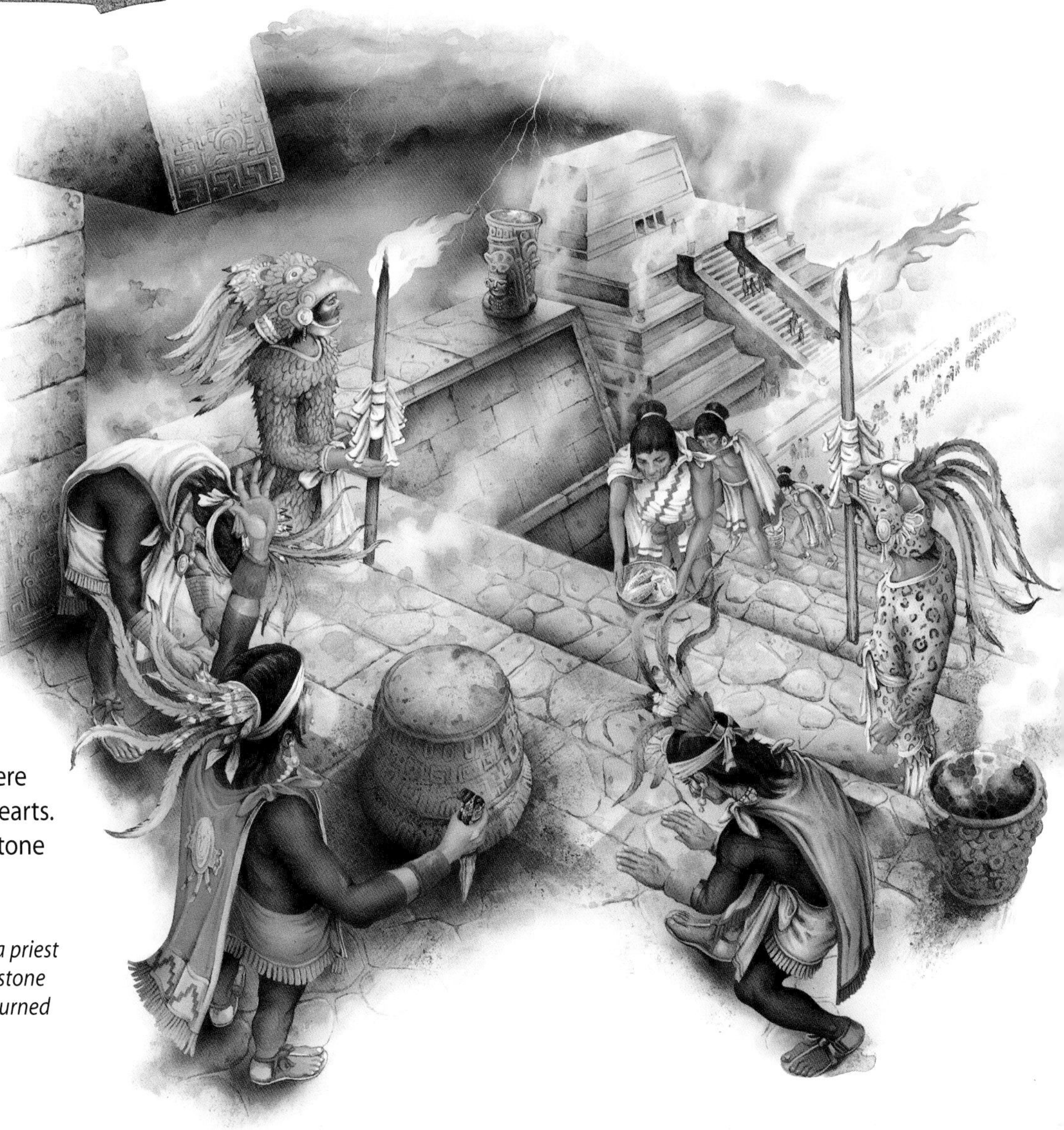

At the top of the Aztec Great Temple, *a priest opened a victim's chest with a sacrificial stone knife. The heart was then removed and burned in a stone bowl.*

***This Buddhist text** of the A.D. 1000's, shows Buddha and a worshiper.*

The Far East

Chinese Deities

Although the constitution of the People's Republic of China grants religious freedom, religious activity is still regulated by the government. When the Communist Party came to power in China, the government tried to discourage religion. During the 1960's and 1970's, many temples and monasteries were destroyed and religious teachers were persecuted. Despite these events, many still continue to keep their religious beliefs. The Chinese believe in a wide variety of deities, demons, gods, and spirits. The dozens of ancient gods have been adopted by the three main religions of China: Taoism, Confucianism, and Buddhism. The Chinese do not believe they have to belong to just one religion. They feel they can attend different temples for different purposes at different times of the year.

***The ceremonial gateway** leads to the temple of Confucius at Qufu in China.*

***The philosopher Confucius,** whose real name was Kong Qiu, founded the system of belief and behavior known as Confucianism.*

Confucianism

Confucianism came about at around the same time as Taoism. Kong Qiu, also called Confucius, believed that people should aim toward achieving peace and order. He taught that the way to do this was for people to respect each other and for each person to work hard to carry out his or her proper roles in society.

Celebrations for Confucius's Birthday

September is celebrated throughout China as the month containing the birthday of Confucius; the precise date of the festival varies with the phases of the moon. The festival begins soon after dawn with ceremonies at the temple, one of which is the ritual pulling of hair from the back of an ox. This hair is then used in sacrificial ceremonies. Hair from the sacred ox is considered to be very lucky, especially for people taking exams. The day continues with dances that are performed on a sacred red carpet. The dances are performed by 64 people arranged in eight rows of eight. The most spectacular celebrations take place in the town of Qufu, where Confucius was born in 551 B.C.

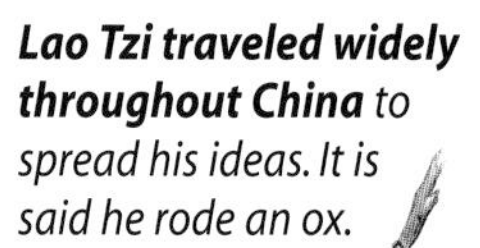

***Lao Tzi traveled widely throughout China** to spread his ideas. It is said he rode an ox.*

THE FAR EAST

The Far East is the easternmost part of Asia. Asia extends from Africa and Europe in the west to the Pacific Ocean in the east. The northernmost part of the continent is in the Arctic. In the south, Asia ends in the tropics near the equator. Traditionally, the term Far East has referred to China, Japan, what are now North Korea and South Korea, Taiwan, and eastern Siberia in Russia. Southeast Asia, which includes Brunei, Cambodia, East Timor, Indonesia, Laos, Malaysia, Myanmar, the Philippines, Singapore, Thailand, and Vietnam, is also often considered part of the Far East.

Taoist Religion in China

Taoism was founded about 2,100 years ago by the scholar Lao Tzi, who taught that humans should work to find harmony with the gods and spirits, as well as with each other. He called this way of living Tao, or "the way." Tao involves carrying out religious duties properly, leading a moral life without committing sin, and living in harmony with other people. Taoists recognize that there are many different gods, as well as humans who have achieved divine status and spirits that roam the earth.

Worship of the Jade emperor

The most important god of the Taoists and of most Chinese people is the Jade emperor, Yu Huang Shang-ti. He is believed to rule over the many different gods, just as the emperor ruled over people on Earth. The Jade emperor decides questions brought to him by the other gods and solves disputes between the gods. Each year, shortly before New Year, the Jade emperor studies the reports brought to him by the spirits and decides if a person deserves to be punished or rewarded in the coming year. He then issues instructions to the gods to bring good luck or bad luck to individual people.

The Jade emperor is shown seated on a throne *and grasping a tablet of jade.*

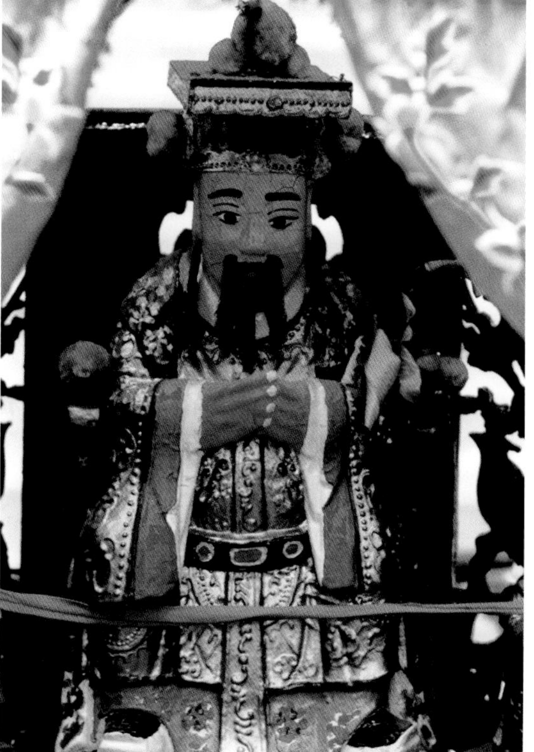

A statue of the Taoist god Pak Tai, *left, prepared for the Cheung Chau Bun Festival on Cheung Chau Island, Hong Kong.*

Cheung Chau Bun Festival

One of the most popular festivals in Hong Kong, southern China, is the Cheung Chau Bun Festival, which is held every year in the spring. The festival is in honor of Pak Tai, the Taoist god of the sea. The fishermen of Cheung Chau pray to Pak Tai for calm weather when they are at sea and also pray in thanks for the way he drove pirates away from the Hong Kong islands. The festival features parades and music, but the highlight comes when the huge stacks of sweet buns, which are sacred to Pak Tai, are handed out to the crowds outside the Taoist temple.

The Birthday of Tam Kung

The god Tam Kung is worshiped among the fishing villages around Hong Kong. He is said to have been a human orphan born centuries ago during the Ching Dynasty. At the age of 12, the boy suddenly acquired the ability to calm storms by throwing peas in the air, to bring rain by throwing water, and generally to control the weather. He became particularly famous for saving the village of Coloane from a terrifying typhoon that destroyed nearby towns. After his death Tam Kung became a god. On his birthday there is a festival in Coloane, and celebrations take place around Macao and Hong Kong. The image of Tam Kung is taken out of his temple and paraded through the streets in a procession that includes people dressed as other gods and immortals. The procession is followed by opera and musical performances. The image of Tam Kung is then taken back to the temple where it remains for a another year.

A colorful procession *takes place in Hong Kong, on the birthday of the god Tam Kung.*

This sacred bronze mirror, symbol of Amaterasu-Omikami, *is located at Amaterasu-Omikami's main temple at Ise. It is considered to be the object in which her spirit dwells during ceremonies and prayers.*

Honoring the Gods of Shinto

The people who follow Shinto, Japan's ancient native religion, worship many deities called kami. The word *Shinto* means the way of the gods. According to Shinto belief, the kami created the world. They dwell in nature, and may live in animals, plants, and in natural places like mountains or rivers. Shinto priests lead ceremonies called matsuri in the dwelling place of a kami. The word *matsuri* is also used to describe the numerous local shrine festivals held in honor of kami all over Japan throughout the year. Almost every shrine has a festival of its own.

An illustration of Amaterasu-Omikami *above Mount Fuji, the home of the gods.*

The Daikoku Matsuri (festival) *is held in honor of the gods of fortune, Daikoku and Ebisu, at the Kanda Myoji Shrine. There are thousands of local festivals throughout Japan dedicated to patron or guardian deities.*

Amaterasu-Omikami

Amaterasu-Omikami, the sun goddess or Queen of Heaven, is regarded as the most important deity of Shinto. According to Shinto mythology, she gave people the gift of culture, wisdom, and light. The Japanese emperor is believed to be a direct descendant of the deity.

Matsuri

Matsuri (festivals) are held to honor the principal gods of local sanctuaries. The whole community participates in the festivities, interrupting their daily activities for the ceremonies to honor the village guardian. During the festival it is believed that the god takes on a material form, such as a plant, stone, mountain, or even a child. The god is welcomed by the people with offerings and prayers.

Deity of the Mountain

One type of kami is the mountain deity known as yama-no-kami. There are many types of yama-no-kami. One type is worshiped by woodsmen and hunters. Another type of yama-no-kami is the deity of agriculture and comes down the mountain during a special time of the year, usually during growing season, to bring good fortune. This kami is honored by farmers who welcome the deity to their fields and seek the deity's intercession for a prosperous crop.

These children are carrying a portable shrine of a mountain god.

A decorated panel called a lamak is made from palm leaves and is decorated with cili, symbols of human fertility. Such panels hang in front of shrines all over Bali during festival time.

Indonesian Celebrations

In Indonesia, there is a complex mix of religions, festivals, and traditions. About 88 percent of Indonesians are Muslims, but there are also communities of Buddhists, Hindus, and Christians, each with its own festivals and traditions. The Indonesian people are made up of several different nations, each of which has its own identity. The diversity of festivals is encouraged by the fact that the population of more than 200 million is spread across 13,000 islands, often separated by wide stretches of ocean.

The Buddhist temple of Borobudur, *built in about A.D. 800, was abandoned when Islam became the chief religion in Indonesia. It was found among the jungle trees in 1814 and has been carefully restored.*

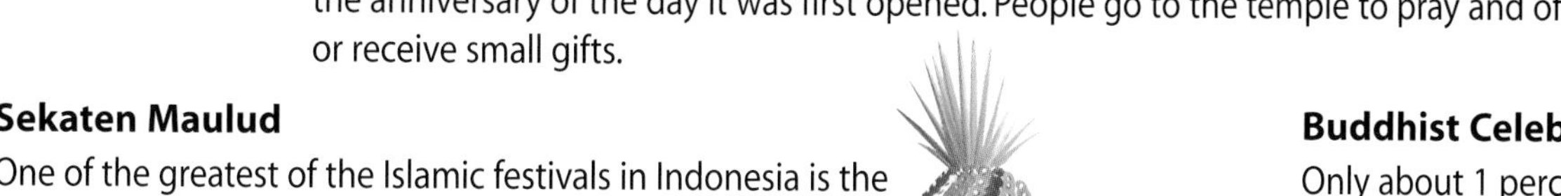

Hindu Holy Days

About 2 percent of the population of Indonesia is Hindu. Most Indonesian Hindus live on Bali and a few other islands in the west. The Hindus have many deities, and each has his or her own festival. One of the most important Hindu festivals on Bali is Galungan. During this festival, people honor deified ancestors and celebrate the victory of good over evil. Hindus erect a bamboo pole called a penjor on which offerings to the gods are suspended. In another religious tradition, each Hindu temple holds a festival on the anniversary of the day it was first opened. People go to the temple to pray and offer or receive small gifts.

Sekaten Maulud

One of the greatest of the Islamic festivals in Indonesia is the Maulud celebration of the birthday of the Prophet Muhammad, who founded the Islamic religion. In Indonesia, it is called the Sekaten Maulud. In some places, the people visit the tombs of famous religious leaders, or gather at the mosque for prayers. In most towns, a procession takes place in which traditional foods are paraded through the streets to the mosque, and then handed out to the faithful who have come to pray. In the town of Yogyakarta, a team of men carry an enormous mound of rice, decorated with cakes and buns, to the mosque for distribution.

Buddhist Celebrations

Only about 1 percent of Indonesians are Buddhist today, but 1,200 years ago the kings of Java were devout Buddhists. They built the vast temple of Borobudur, which is made of an entire hill carved into the shape of a temple. The building has recently been restored and is used for important Buddhist festivals, including Wesak, the birthday of Buddha.

The great dish of rice and cakes, *known as gunungan wadon, is carried through the streets of Yogyakarta on the birthday of the Prophet Muhammad.*

Wesak, Buddha's Birthday

Buddhist festivals are almost always held at the full moon, *so the exact date varies from year to year, depending on the phases of the moon.*

Buddhism is a religion followed by millions of people in Asia and elsewhere. The founder of Buddhism was an Indian prince named Siddhartha Gautama who lived about 2,500 years ago. At the age of 29, Siddhartha left his luxurious palace to wander the countryside in search of religious enlightenment. After six years he came to Bihar, where he suddenly realized the purpose of human existence. After this he was known as Buddha, which means "the enlightened one." Buddha spent the rest of his life teaching other people about his beliefs and the ways in which he thought people should lead their lives. He passed away at the age of about 80.

***Before Buddha was born, his mother dreamed of a giant white elephant** and interpreted this to mean she would give birth to a great hero.*

Buddha's Birth

After Buddha's death many stories were told about his birth and childhood, though it is unclear how many of these stories were known while he lived. Siddhartha was the son of King Suddhodhana and Queen Maya, who dreamed of a sacred white elephant before the birth.

A monk prays before a large statue of Buddha resting.

Wesak

The most important festival in the Buddhist religion is Wesak, which occurs on the day of a full moon in the spring. Wesak is a commemoration of the day on which Buddha was born, the day he achieved enlightenment, and the day on which he died. In most Asian countries, Wesak is a public holiday so that worshipers can attend the temple rituals or take part in the many ceremonies which are held to mark this important day. In some countries, Wesak is known as Visakha or Buddha Purinama.

***In Vietnam and Malaysia, Buddhist monks** release thousands of captive birds at Wesak to show kindness and compassion for all things.*

A grand parade of children *takes place to celebrate Wesak in Tokyo.*

During Wesak, worshipers dressed in pure white light incense sticks *placed in a bowl shaped like a sacred lotus flower.*

Celebrating Wesak

The holy day of Wesak is celebrated in various ways in different countries, but everywhere it is a time of celebration and of reflection. The day begins at dawn when gongs and drums are sounded in the temples. Devout Buddhists dress in pure white and walk to the temple where they sit quietly to think about the Eightfold Path of Buddha, which includes the instruction to abstain from killing and to abstain from stealing, as well as to avoid evil thoughts. Monks and priests may spend the entire day in a temple contemplating these ideas. Outside the temple there are parades, fairs, and dances. Wealthy people may set up a stall from which they give food and drink free to anyone who passes by, or they may hand out scrolls and books on which are written the teachings of Buddha. After sunset, special lanterns are lit outside houses and temples. The holy books are read quietly, or monks may retell the stories about Buddha's life and his message to humanity.

Japanese children *wear special clothes decorated with flowers at Wesak.*

BUDDHA IMAGES

In the years after Buddha passed away, his followers began creating images of Buddha at his work. Many statues of Buddha show him seated, teaching his views to his followers. The positions of the statue's hands symbolize different aspects of Buddha's message. Some statues show Buddha lying down with his eyes partially open. This is a depiction of Buddha as he passed away to enter nirvana, the state of perfect existence which all Buddhists hope to attain. This statue with two heads shows Buddha's compassion. Two Chinese Buddhists were too poor to afford a statue each, so they bought one to share. Buddha miraculously divided the statue so that each man had an image of Buddha.

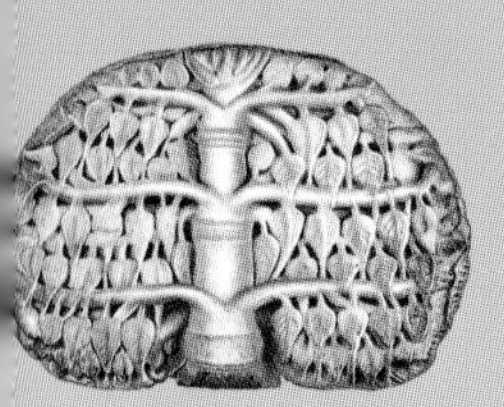

The sacred Bodhi tree, *under which Buddha sat and became enlightened, is depicted in this image. The actual tree, in India, is a place of pilgrimage for Buddhists.*

Other Buddhist Celebrations

Buddhist festivals are celebrated at different times and in different ways, depending on how Buddhism has merged with local cultural traditions. In many parts of south and central Asia, Buddhists hold big celebrations to remember Buddha's life and his enlightenment. Buddha's death, when he passed into nirvana, is marked by another festival, Paranirvana. Other festivals mark religious events in Buddha's life, or center on relics of Buddha. In Kandy, Sri Lanka, there is a special procession to honor the sacred tooth of Buddha.

Siddhartha Gautama *left the comforts of the palace to follow the example of a holy man, who was happy despite being poor.*

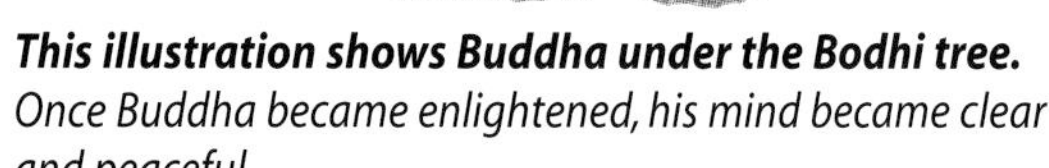

This illustration shows Buddha under the Bodhi tree. *Once Buddha became enlightened, his mind became clear and peaceful.*

Buddha's Search for Enlightenment

Buddha was born a nobleman. As a young man he gave up his privileged life to become a holy man and search for the truth. He spent many years traveling around northern India leading a rough life, eating little, and meditating for hours at a time. One evening he sat to meditate under a spreading Bodhi tree. During that night he finally realized the truth about life and became Buddha (Enlightened One).

Buddha *is depicted as peacefully passing away, with his followers around him.*

Nirvana

When Buddha was about 80, his work in the world was done, and he died. Buddhists believe that he entered nirvana, a place of complete peace. His body was cremated (burned), and his relics were placed in special buildings called stupas. These were shrines that Buddhists could visit to remember Buddha.

SOUTH AND CENTRAL ASIA

South and Central Asia are areas of distinct cultures and peoples. These regions form an area at the base of Asia. Asia extends from Africa and Europe in the west to the Pacific Ocean in the east. The northernmost part of the continent is in the Arctic. In the south, Asia ends in the tropics near the equator. South Asia is made up of Afghanistan, Bangladesh, Bhutan, India, the Maldives, Nepal, Pakistan, Sri Lanka, and the Tibetan plateau in southwest China. Much of India, the largest country in South Asia, forms a peninsula that extends southward into the Indian Ocean. Central Asia includes Kazakhstan, Kyrgyzstan, Mongolia, Tajikistan, Turkmenistan, Uzbekistan, and the West Siberian Plain in Russia.

Poson Day

At Poson, Buddhists celebrate the coming of Buddhism to Sri Lanka. In 247 B.C., Arahat Mahinda, the son of the Indian emperor, convinced the king of Sri Lanka to become a Buddhist, and his country adopted the religion. On Poson Day, Buddhists from Sri Lanka go to the temple. The Buddhist flag is raised outside the building as everybody watches. People gather inside the temple to hear a talk about Mahinda's arrival in Sri Lanka. They chant and meditate, and make offerings. Later a delicious Sri Lankan meal is shared.

A statue of Buddha at the temple in Mihintale, Sri Lanka, right, *marks the sacred site where Buddhism started in Sri Lanka.*

Buddhist offerings of candles and flowers *are shown in a temple. The candles are a symbol of Buddha's teaching, which lights up the world.*

Celebrating Nirvana

At the Paranirvana festival, Buddhists remember Buddha's death. At the temple they listen to readings about Buddha's last days in this world. They may meditate in dim light. Buddhists teach that it is important to accept loss and not to grieve and experience pain. As well as remembering Buddha's death, they take the opportunity to think about their own future death and remember loved ones who have died recently. Special prayers are said for people who are dying, in the hope that their next life will be good.

This Tibetan bronze statue depicts a stupa, *an important place of worship.*

The "Sacred Tooth" of Kandy

The sacred tooth of Buddha is a famous relic, housed in its own special temple in Kandy, Sri Lanka. It is said that the tooth was brought to the island in the 300's. A joyful parade is held every July or August, involving hundreds of elephants. The chief elephant carries the golden stupa that contains a replica of the tooth. The actual tooth is never seen, as it is kept in the temple.

The sacred tooth festival is special to Sri Lanka, *and many local people join the elephants in this spectacular procession.*

Janmashtami, Krishna's Birthday

Hindus believe in one god, Brahman, who has no form and cannot be seen but is present in all things. Each of the many Hindu deities represents an aspect of Brahman. The principal deities are Brahma, Vishnu, and Shiva. According to Hindus, Krishna is an avatar (physical form) of Vishnu, who comes to Earth to protect the good people, punish the wicked, and restore true religion. There are 10 avatars of Vishnu, and Krishna is one of the most popular. He reminds people of the love between Brahman and human beings. Janmashtami is a joyful Hindu festival to celebrate the birth of Lord Krishna. It takes place on the anniversary of Krishna's birth in August/September. For some Hindus, this is the most important festival of the year.

***The cow goddess* Kamadhenu** *grants all wishes and is the mother of all cows. In Hinduism, all cows are considered sacred because they are the givers of milk and are associated with Krishna, the milk-loving god.*

Krishna is often shown as a young boy, *above right, dipping his hands in milk or butter; it is said that he loved dairy foods.*

Chariots and Battle

The *Bhagavad-Gita* is a long poem in the *Mahabharata*. Within it is a discussion between Krishna and the warrior Arjuna that takes place on the battlefield. The battle is between good and evil, action and inaction, and between knowledge and ignorance. Krishna persuades Arjuna into action and becomes his charioteer. After many battles both armies are almost completely destroyed. Krishna is one of the few survivors but he dies soon after. While meditating in a forest, a hunter mistakes him for a deer and shoots him with a fatal arrow. At his death, Krishna rises to heaven where he is greeted by the gods.

***This image from the* Bhagavad-Gita** *shows Krishna driving the chariot, with Arjuna the warrior inside.*

Krishna

There are many exciting stories about Krishna told in the famous Hindu book the Mahabharata. It is said that the god Vishnu was persuaded to come to Earth in the form of the avatar Krishna because demons were about to overcome the gods. The demon-king, Kamsa, planned to kill Krishna as a little baby. But when the baby was born, his father swapped him for another woman's baby girl. When Kamsa came to kill Krishna, he found this baby girl, who miraculously escaped when he tried to murder her. Later in life, Krishna challenged Kamsa and killed him.

This procession is part of the Janmashtami festival *in Rajasthan, India. Hindus also visit the temple for worship.*

Celebrating Janmashtami

On the festival day, people decorate their homes and temples to welcome the birth of Krishna, and they may fast. An image of the newborn Krishna is placed on a swing in the temple. At midnight, the image is bathed in charnamrita—curd (milk solids) mixed with milk, dry fruit, and leaves. The arati ceremony is then performed. Lamps are moved in circles in front of the image of Krishna, and people sing religious songs. By now everyone is hungry. They break their fast with a sweet called prasad, and may then eat a delicious Indian meal.

These children in Bangladesh have their faces painted to celebrate Janmashtami. *Krishna is usually shown with a blue face.*

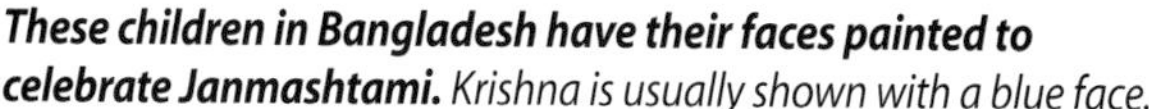

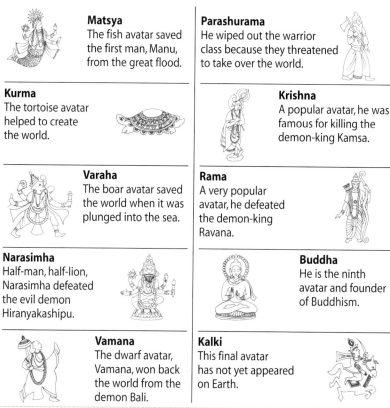

THE TEN AVATARS OF VISHNU

These illustrations show the 10 avatars (physical forms) of Vishnu. Hindus believe that Kalki, the 10th avatar, will come on a white horse and destroy all evil.

Matsya
The fish avatar saved the first man, Manu, from the great flood.

Kurma
The tortoise avatar helped to create the world.

Varaha
The boar avatar saved the world when it was plunged into the sea.

Narasimha
Half-man, half-lion, Narasimha defeated the evil demon Hiranyakashipu.

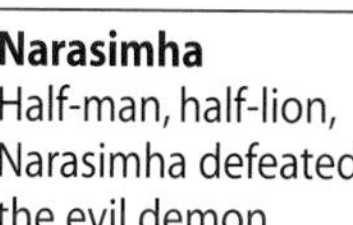

Vamana
The dwarf avatar, Vamana, won back the world from the demon Bali.

Parashurama
He wiped out the warrior class because they threatened to take over the world.

Krishna
A popular avatar, he was famous for killing the demon-king Kamsa.

Rama
A very popular avatar, he defeated the demon-king Ravana.

Buddha
He is the ninth avatar and founder of Buddhism.

Kalki
This final avatar has not yet appeared on Earth.

A group of young men build a human pyramid *to reach the pot filled with dairy treats, during Janmashtami festivities in the streets of Mumbai.*

Dahi-Handi

According to legend, as a child, Krishna and his friends would enter the houses of milkmaids to steal milk and butter, Krishna's favorite treat. The Dahi-Handi ceremony, performed in the streets of India during Janmashtami, commemorates Krishna and his love for milk and butter. A pot filled with milk, butter, and other milk products is hung high above the street. Young people build human pyramids to try to reach and break the pot, just as Krishna and his friends would have done. Prize money, along with the contents of the pot, is then awarded to the group who reaches the top.

Navaratri and Dussehra

Gauri is the local form of the goddess Parvati in Rajasthan. *At the Gangaur festival, women honor Gauri, the goddess of abundance.*

The Hindu mother goddess takes on many forms. The main form of the goddess is Lord Shiva's companion, often called Durga. Durga, known as the destroyer of evil, also has many forms. She can be terrifying and destructive as Kali, or kind and gentle as Parvati. The festivals to commemorate the goddess have different names in different parts of India—Dussehra and Navaratri are just two of them. The celebrations, which last 9 to 10 days, vary from place to place and are also linked to the harvest. In the Punjab region of northern India, a fast is followed by feasting, while in Gujarat, 9 nights of the festival are celebrated with the performance of special dances.

The goddess Durga *is often shown riding a lion or a tiger to illustrate her strength.*

The Goddess Durga

The goddess is a very important form of god in Hinduism. Durga is powerful. She is so strong that she can control a lion or tiger. She carries weapons for killing the buffalo demon that threatens the world. This demon is a symbol for ignorance. As Kali, the goddess is absolutely terrifying. She often appears hideous, wild, and violent; she has many heads and her tongue drips with blood. Kali has huge power to destroy evil and for this she receives great devotion. At Dussehra, one of the most popular festivals in India, the goddess Durga is worshiped as the divine mother.

Kali is the most violent form of the goddess Durga. *Goddesses are sometimes companions to the gods; at other times they act alone.*

MANGO SORBET

- 4 egg whites
- 1 lb. mango pulp
- 1/2 teaspoon lemon juice
- grated rind of 1 lemon
- grated rind of 1 orange
- 1/4 cup superfine sugar

In a medium bowl, beat the egg whites with an electric mixer at high speed until stiff peaks form. Set this aside. In a large, cold bowl, mix together the mango pulp, lemon juice, and orange and lemon rinds. Gradually stir in the sugar. Then gently fold in the egg whites. Cover with plastic wrap and freeze one hour. Remove from freezer and beat with mixer again, for about one minute. Transfer to an ice-cream container and freeze until firm.

ACCORDING TO LEGEND, mango is one of the oldest fruits cultivated in India. It is believed that Shiva brought mango to India for his wife Parvati, the kind and gentle goddess.

***At Dussehra, in parts of India, people act out the story of Rama's victory** over the demon Ravana in processions.*

Celebrating Dussehra

In northern India, the festival to worship the mother goddess is called Dussehra. It is celebrated for 10 days around late September and early October. People place images of the goddess in their homes and public places. In Gujarat, the festival is called Navaratri (Nine Nights). On the 10th day, Hindus immerse the images of Durga in the river.

***A statue of Durga and other deities** is taken out to the Ranjit River. The statue is in Darjeeling, a town in the West Bengal state of northern India.*

Storytelling and Worship

At Dussehra, Hindus perform puja (worship), listen to religious music, and hear traditional stories describing the talents and power of the mother goddess. The storyteller explains the meaning to the audience. In northern India, Dussehra is linked to the story of the Ramayana. People use giant puppets to act out the story of Rama's fight with the 10-headed demon Ravana. On the 10th day, the puppet of Ravana is filled with fireworks and burned.

The Stick Dance

At the Gujarati festival of Navaratri, everyone dances around a special shrine made from a box. On each side of the box is a picture of the mother goddess in one of her forms. There are two traditional dances, a garba (circle dance) and dandiya ras (stick dance). The dancing and singing start in the evening and continue into the night. Some people attend the celebrations for each of the nine nights.

***These men and women take part in the dandiya ras (stick dance).** Participating in the nine-day festival helps to strengthen the feeling of community among Hindus.*

NAVARATRI IS ALSO KNOWN AS DURGA PUJA. It takes place during the first 10 days of Ashwin, one of the 12 months of the Hindu lunar calendar. The month of Ashwin falls between mid-September and mid-October of the Gregorian calendar. The festival ends with Dussehra, which means 10th day.

A sandstone sculpture of the god Shiva *in the form of the Lord of the Ganas, a dwarf. Shiva was the father of Ganesa.*

Ganesa Chaturthi, Ganesa's Birthday

Ganesa is a popular elephant-headed god worshiped by Hindus all over India. Many families have a murti (image) of Ganesa on their shrine at home. In India, elephants have traditionally been used to remove obstacles, such as tree trunks. Hindus worship Ganesa when they have a problem or a challenge to face, such as moving to a new house or going on a trip. The 10-day festival of Ganesa, called Ganesa Chaturthi, falls in August or September. It is believed that praying to Ganesa during the festival brings good luck and prosperity.

The image of Ganesa *is an embodiment of wisdom.*

The Festivities

Before Ganesa Chaturthi, Hindus make or buy murtis of Ganesa for their shrine. They decorate the murtis with flower garlands and lights and pray to them. Huge images are displayed in public places. At the end of the festival, the crowds take the images down to the sea or river and plunge them into the water.

The Elephant God

It is said that one day Parvati, Lord Shiva's wife, created Ganesa out of dirt. She told him to guard the door while she bathed. When Shiva returned, he thought that Ganesa was a stranger and cut off his head. His wife Parvati demanded that Shiva return her son to life. Shiva cut off the head of the first creature he saw—which happened to be an elephant—and fitted it onto Ganesa.

Ganesa is known for his love of laddus, *a sweet made from sugar and nuts. This man, left, sells laddus to worshipers to offer to Ganesa.*

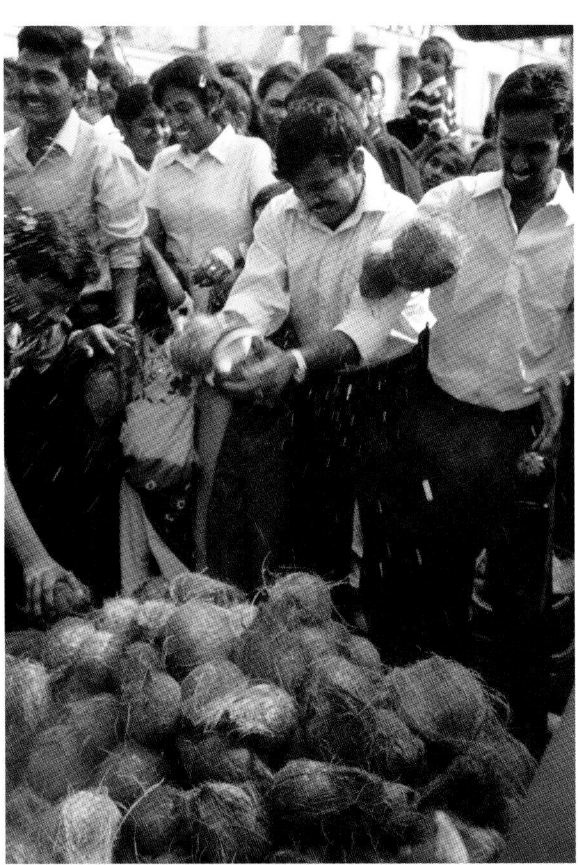

A group of men break coconuts at the Ganesa festival, right. *Ganesa once saw the moon's reflection and thought it was a coconut.*

Mistaking the Moon

In parts of southern India, Hindus believe it is unlucky to look at the moon on the day that the images of Ganesa are plunged into water. According to myth, Ganesa once saw the moon reflected in a pool of water. A great food lover, he thought it was a coconut and tried to pick it up. The moon laughed at him. Ganesa was offended; he cursed the moon and all those who saw the moon that day.

THE WORD *CHATURTHI* MEANS FOURTH DAY. The festival Ganesa Chaturthi falls on the fourth day of the month of the Bhadrapada of the Hindu calendar.

Guru Nanak's Birthday

Guru Nanak was the founder of Sikhism, so his birthday is one of the most important Sikh festivals. After Guru Nanak, there were nine other gurus. The anniversaries of all their births and deaths are celebrated. Just before Guru Nanak's birthday, Sikhs take turns to read their holy book, the *Guru Granth Sahib*, all the way through. This takes about 48 hours. On his birthday, Sikhs hear how Guru Nanak started their religion, and then they enjoy a tasty shared meal.

Some Sikhs use prayer beads called mala *to help them focus on prayer.*

This illustration shows Guru Nanak seated between his friends. *Guru Nanak is usually depicted with a halo around his head and seated in a cross-legged position.*

Guru Nanak

Guru Nanak was born in India in A.D. 1469. At the time, the main religions in India were Hinduism and Islam. Guru Nanak did not agree with some aspects of the Hindu religion, such as the caste system. The caste system divided people into fixed classes according to their family's trade. Guru Nanak heard the call of God. He left his job as a government official. The guru became a religious teacher, traveling around and gathering followers around him. Guru Nanak believed that there was one God. People could serve God by doing their duty and working for the good of society as a whole. He taught that all people were equal whatever their class, race, or gender. The guru believed that all people should be free to follow their chosen religion. Before he died, Guru Nanak named one of his followers to be the next guru.

These verses from the Guru Granth Sahib, *the Sikh holy scriptures, are engraved above the entrance to the Golden Temple in Amritsar, India.*

Setting an Example

It is said that Guru Nanak spent many years traveling around India, Sri Lanka, and Tibet teaching his message. Eventually in 1521, Guru Nanak and his family settled down in Kartarpur in the present-day Indian state of Punjab. The guru established a religious center and devoted the rest of his life to serving the community. He established the tradition of gathering to worship and sing hymns.

These Sikh girls *are in traditional costume: kameez (dress), salwar (trousers), and dupatta (scarf).*

A compass is often carried by devout Muslims so that wherever they are, they can make sure they pray in the direction of Mecca.

The Middle East

Muhammad's Birthday

Muslims believe that Muhammad was the last of the many prophets who brought the message of Allah (God) to the world. They believe that he was the perfect prophet, and they try to follow his example. It is not known exactly when Muhammad was born, but his birthday is usually celebrated on the 12th day of the third month, Rabi' al-Awwal. It was first celebrated in the A.D. 1200's, and the custom quickly spread throughout the Islamic world. There are prayers and gatherings during the month of Muhammad's birth. In some places, the festival is quite solemn because the date also marks the anniversary of the prophet's death. Some groups of Muslims do not celebrate Muhammad's birthday at all.

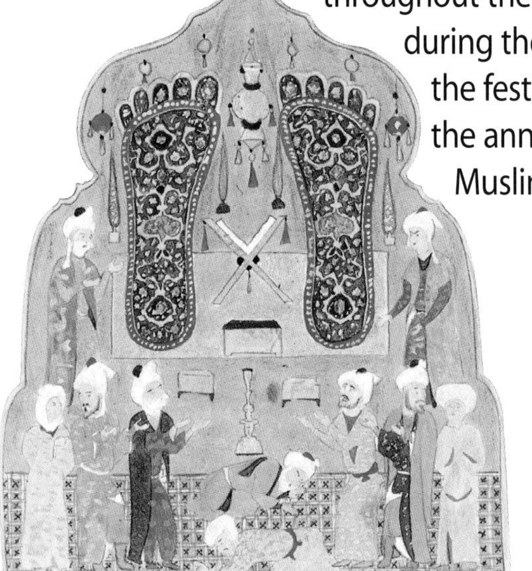

This illustration shows Muslims honoring the Qur'ān and footprints of Muhammad.

The Early Prophets

The roots of Islam lie with Adam, the first man, according to religious tradition. Muslims believe that he was the first of many prophets, sent by Allah to show people how to behave in the world and how to worship him as the one God. The Qur'ān mentions 25 prophets, many of whom also appear in the Jewish Torah and the Christian Bible. They include Ibrahim (Abraham), Musa (Moses), and Isa (Jesus). Allah kept sending new prophets, but people did not keep to their teachings.

THE PROPHET ABRAHAM

Although there is some disagreement about the life of the prophet Abraham (called Ibrahim by Muslims), he is revered by Muslims, Jews, and Christians. According to the Bible, Abraham left his home in Mesopotamia on God's instructions. God made a covenant, or promise to Abraham, telling him that he would make him the founder of a great nation. Abraham obeyed God with an unquestioning faith, even to the point of sacrificing his own son (see page 27). The Jewish people consider Abraham the first patriarch, or founder of the Hebrew nation. For Muslims, he is the builder of the first shrine to the One True God.

Abraham left Mesopotamia, as God had commanded, *and led the members of his clan to the land God had shown him.*

THE MIDDLE EAST

The Middle East covers parts of northern Africa, southwestern Asia, and southeastern Europe. Scholars disagree on which countries make up the Middle East. But many say the region consists of Bahrain, Cyprus, Egypt, Iran, Iraq, Israel, Jordan, Kuwait, Lebanon, Oman, Qatar, Saudi Arabia, Sudan, Syria, Turkey, United Arab Emirates, and Yemen. The region also is the birthplace of three major religions–Christianity, Islam, and Judaism.

The Early Life of Muhammad

The Prophet Muhammad was born in about A.D. 570 and grew up in Mecca, Saudi Arabia. He was brought up by his grandfather and his uncle. An honest, hard-working man, he married a wealthy widow, Khadija, when he was 25. Muhammad spent much time in prayer looking for spiritual guidance. At about age 40, he received his first message from Allah, through the angel Jibril (Gabriel).

This illustration shows the birth of Muhammad *in a miniature from the A.D. 1500's from the Ottoman Empire. His mother died when he was a young boy.*

Battles and Struggles

Muhammad began to preach Allah's message in public. He taught that there was one God and that all human beings were equal. Muhammad fought corruption and helped poor people. However, as Muhammad gained followers, the rulers of Mecca began to see him as a threat. It became dangerous for the Muslims, as they were now known, to stay in Mecca. They were invited to move to Medina, and the prophet became the ruler there. The people of Mecca were still determined to oppose the Muslims, and there were several fierce battles between them. Finally in A.D. 630, Muhammad overcame Mecca. He was a lenient and forgiving conqueror.

Muhammad's followers rode into battle *against the people of Mecca. The prophet eventually marched on Mecca with 10,000 men and defeated his enemies.*

The Dome of the Rock mosque in Jerusalem *is the spot from which Muhammad is believed to have risen into heaven one night. In heaven, Muhammad is believed to have met all the other prophets.*

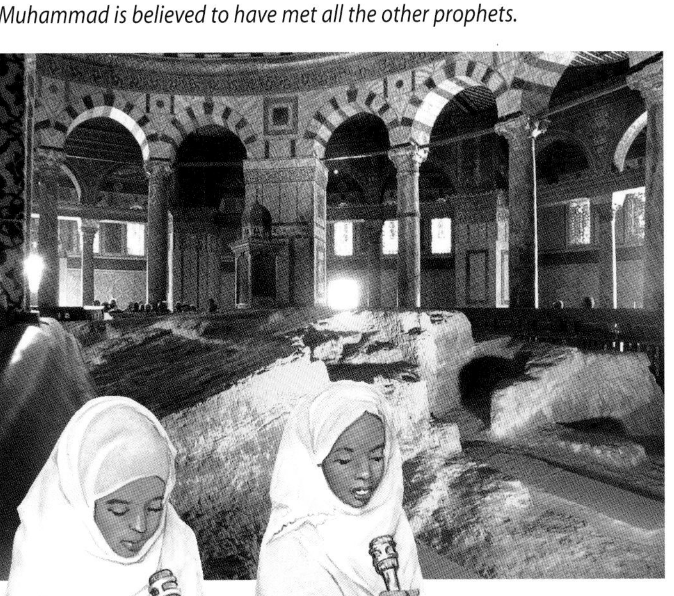

The Death of Muhammad

In A.D. 632, the Prophet Muhammad realized that his mission in the world was coming to an end. He went on a pilgrimage to Mecca and addressed the crowds with an emotional sermon. Upon returning to Medina he fell ill. He died in the arms of his youngest wife, Aishah, and was buried in the room where he died. His grave remains a place of pilgrimage.

This painting shows the grief of Muhammad's followers *at the loss of their leader. The next leader of the Muslims was Abu Bakr.*

These girls are reciting from the Qur'ān *as part of a competition on the prophet's birthday.*

Muslim children wave flags *as they take part in a festival procession to celebrate Muhammad's life.*

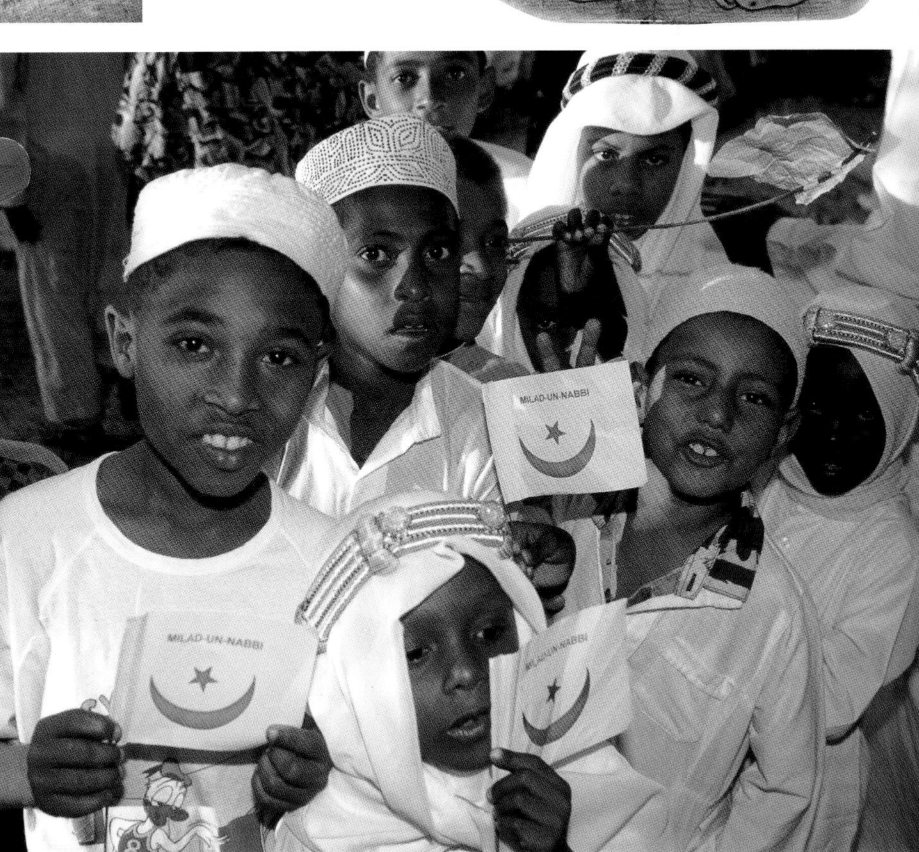

Celebrating Mawlid

At this festival, Muslims gather in mosques to remember the prophet's birth and life. In some countries, people decorate mosques and public buildings with bright bunting and flags. During the ceremony they hear about Muhammad's life and thank Allah for giving them the example of the prophet to follow. Feasts of meat and rice are arranged, and food is shared with the poor.

The Month of Hajj and Celebrating Ibrahim

*This painting **celebrating the Hajj** shows a man with his camel on the way to Mecca. Today most people fly to the holy site.*

Performing the Hajj, the pilgrimage to Mecca, is a duty that all Muslims try to fulfill at least once in their lifetime. Visiting the city of Mecca in Saudi Arabia and other holy sites, along with millions of other Muslims, is a deeply religious experience. The true Hajj must be made between the 8th and 13th of Dhul-Hijja, the 12th month of the Muslim calendar. The feast of 'Id al-Adha is the climax of the pilgrimage month and one of the most important festivals of the Islamic year. It celebrates Ibrahim's (Abraham's) faith in the face of temptation by the devil and his obedience to the will of Allah.

Going on the Hajj

According to the Qur'ān, people may go on the Hajj only if they are healthy and their family is well provided for. Today, about 2 million people from countries all around the world make the pilgrimage. Before they enter Mecca, pilgrims change into simple clothing so that they all appear equal before Allah. Male pilgrims wear two sheets of unsewn white cloth and women wear a plain long-sleeved white robe. There are various rituals undertaken by all the pilgrims in and around Mecca.

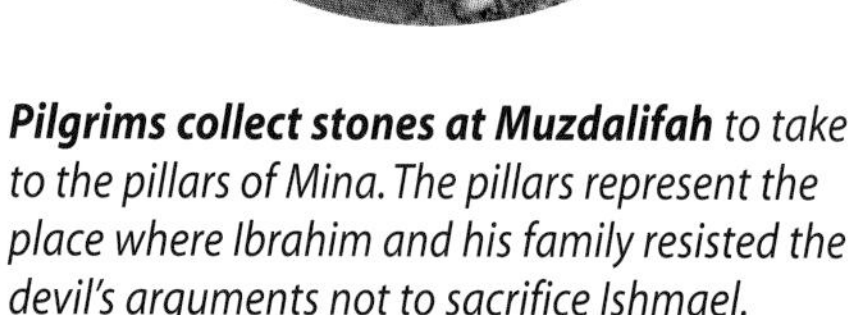

***Pilgrims collect stones at Muzdalifah** to take to the pillars of Mina. The pillars represent the place where Ibrahim and his family resisted the devil's arguments not to sacrifice Ishmael.*

***Pilgrims pray and listen to a sermon on Mount Arafat,** where Muhammad gave his last sermon.*

Driving the Devil Away

First, all pilgrims circle the Kaaba, the cube-shaped shrine to Allah in the Great Mosque in Mecca. At Muzdalifah, an encampment near Mina, pilgrims pick up pebbles to hurl at the pillars of Mina. At Mina, the devil tried to persuade Ibrahim not to follow Allah's command to sacrifice Ishmael (Isaac). In memory of how Ibrahim's family stoned the devil to drive him away, the pilgrims throw stones at the pillars. Then they head for the plain of Arafat, where they stand in the baking heat from midday to sunset, focusing on God alone.

Ibrahim prepared to sacrifice his son Ishmael. *At the last moment, Allah provided a ram instead.*

A woman pours Zamzam water *collected from a well on the grounds of the courtyard of the Great Mosque. The well of Zamzam is where Ishmael's mother found water for them to drink. People drink it and take some home with them.*

Testing Beliefs

Ibrahim's only son, Ishmael, was born when his parents were already elderly. One day, Ibrahim saw a vision in which he was killing Ishmael. He was convinced that Allah was telling him to kill the boy as a sacrifice to him. The boy understood and said that if this was the will of Allah, then it should be done. Just as the father was about to kill his son, Allah provided a ram for sacrifice instead. Ibrahim had passed the test of his faith.

Feast of the Sacrifice

At 'Id al-Adha, Muslims celebrate Ibrahim's faith in the will of Allah. In Muslim countries, it is a four-day holiday. On the first day of the feast, people rise early, wash, and put on fresh, clean clothes. They go to the mosque to pray. Everyone thinks about the pilgrims who are on Hajj; today they can watch the events on TV. An animal such as a sheep or goat is sacrificed in the proper humane way. A large share is offered to poor Muslims; sometimes it is the only occasion on which they eat meat.

Most Muslims sacrifice a goat *or sheep at 'Id al-Adha, but a camel is sometimes used. The meat from a camel can feed up to seven families.*

Pilgrims walk around a black cube called the Kaaba 7 times.

Building of the Kaaba

The Kaaba was built by Ibrahim and Ishmael. It was a square-walled sanctuary with a flat roof. This simple building became a holy place of pilgrimage.

The Month of Ramadan

Ramadan is a special month for Muslims, because it was during this time that the Prophet Muhammad received his first message from Allah. The messages make up the Qur'ān, the holy book that provides guidance to Muslims. The ninth month of the Muslim calendar, Ramadan, can occur in all the seasons. The calendar is made up of 12 lunar months. It is 354 days long, 12 days shorter than the Western calendar. The Muslim festivals, therefore, move backward through the Western calendar each year. Nearly all practicing Muslims fast during Ramadan. Lailat ul-Qadr is during the last 10 nights of Ramadan. Many Muslims attend the mosque on all 10 nights. It is believed that on Lailat ul-Qadr the angels come down to Earth, bringing special blessings for true worshipers of Allah.

A silver hand symbolizes the Five Pillars of Islam. *Sawm (fasting) is the fourth pillar. Each pillar is seen as part of the supporting structure of the religion, helping to provide a firm foundation for people's beliefs.*

A family breaks the Ramadan fast at sunset *with just a small amount of food. A full meal follows later.*

Fasting in the Month of Ramadan

Muslims fast from dawn to sunset for the entire month of Ramadan. Nothing must pass their lips—no food, water, or even chewing gum—during this time. Fasting helps to focus the mind, body, and spirit on Allah alone. There is a great sense of unity in sharing the fast with Muslims all over the world. All healthy adult Muslims should take part. Children under the age of puberty, pregnant women, the elderly, and sick people need not fast. Those excused occasionally from fasting are expected to make up the missed fast days later. The food that is eaten to break the fast at the end of the day is called iftar. It usually consists of a few dates and a drink of water. Later on, families and friends gather for a proper meal. Every night, some large city mosques offer an evening meal to hundreds of Muslims. They make sure that poor people, travelers, and those who live alone enjoy a good meal after fasting all day.

QURĀN MEANS RECITATION. The Qur'ān is the Islamic holy book, which was gradually revealed to Muhammad through Allah's messenger, Jibril. Muslims believe that the Qur'ān is the word of Allah; it was received through Muhammad but not written by him. The Qur'ān was intended to be heard, and it is believed that blessings flow from listening to it. Muslims are taught to recite from the Qur'ān, and they must always learn it in the original Arabic.

Lailat ul-Qadr

Muhammad spent his life seeking spiritual guidance. One day, when he was 40 years old, he went to pray in a cave on Mount Hira, near Mecca. It is said that suddenly he heard a voice call out his name, commanding "Recite." The angel Jibril (Gabriel) appeared to him. Muhammad saw words but replied that he could not read. Three times the angel ordered him to read aloud. After the third time, Muhammad, to his amazement, began to recite what became the first words of the Qur'ān. This night became known as Lailat ul-Qadr (the Night of Power). Muhammad continued to receive revelations and to teach them to others for the rest of his life.

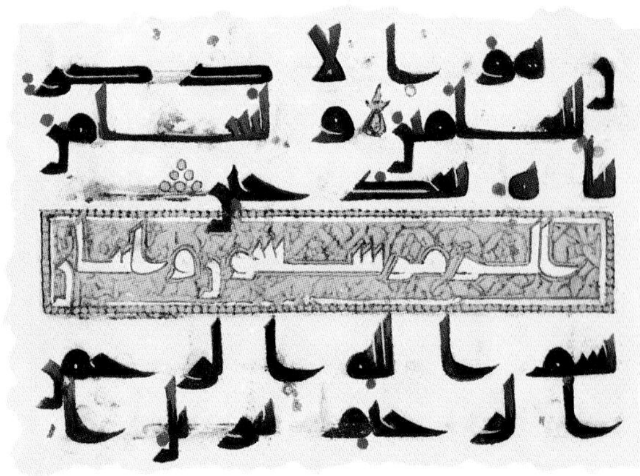

This manuscript of the Qur'ān, *written in the ancient Kufic script, is decorated with gold. The angel Jibril first revealed Allah's words—which became the Qur'ān—to Muhammad on Lailat ul-Qadr.*

Celebrating the End of Ramadan

Ramadan ends on the morning after the new moon is sighted, signaling the start of the next month. On the night when the new moon is expected, people often crowd into the streets, looking out for the sign that Ramadan is over. The following morning is the first day of *'Id al-Fitr,* which means breaking of the fast. This festival is a time to celebrate the good things people have received from Allah and to be grateful for family and friends. At 'Id al-Fitr, grudges and bad feelings are forgotten. 'Id al-Fitr has a fixed routine. Muslims have a bath or shower and put on their best clothes. They eat a simple breakfast, and then they attend a gathering in the largest mosque or outdoors. They pray and then greet each other. Everyone says "Id Mubarak"—"Happy Festival." Then the round of visits begins.

'Id al-Fitr is a happy and joyous occasion for both young and old. *'Id al-Fitr and 'Id al-Adha, which occurs about 10 weeks later, are the major Islamic festivals.*

Praying

The 'Id al-Fitr prayers are held in very large mosques or in large open areas. Muslims offer prayers of thanksgiving to Allah for his help at the end of the month of fasting. On this occasion, people wear white gowns over their normal clothes. This is so that they appear equal before Allah. As well as the five daily prayers, there is also a special 'Id al-Fitr prayer that is said after sunset.

During prayer, Muslims bow to the ground, above left, *to show reverence and submission to Allah.*

Celebrations

Many Muslims like to put up decorations for 'Id al-Fitr. This has to be done at the last minute, when the moon has been spotted. Special foods are prepared for the celebration meal. These vary from country to country. There are some typical cakes called mamoul. Made from a dough of semolina (wheat flour), dates, and pistachio nuts (or walnuts), they are pressed into a mold to make little round balls. Also typical are labaneh, small balls of dried yogurt, eaten with bread and thyme. Children love this festival. They often receive money and other presents, as well as sweets and nuts.

The custom of sending other Muslims Happy 'Id al-Fitr cards *is a custom that is growing in popularity.*

IN MUSLIM COUNTRIES, THERE IS A THREE-DAY HOLIDAY FOR 'ID AL-FITR, so there is plenty of time for visiting friends and relatives. People will visit different branches of the family on different days. In non-Muslim countries, people take the day off from work or school. As well as visiting relatives in their homes, there may be festivities in the streets, including fairs, the sale of sweets, and fireworks displays.

A mold is used to make mamoul, *delicious 'Id al-Fitr treats.*

The Báb and Bahá'u'lláh

The Bahá'í faith is the youngest world religion. Bahá'ís regard their prophet Bahá'u'lláh as the most recent messenger of God. Other messengers have included Abraham, Moses, Buddha, Zoroaster, Jesus, and Muhammad. The religion originated when Siyyid 'Alí Muhammad claimed to be a new prophet, calling himself the Báb. After the Báb's death, a new messenger, the Bahá'u'lláh, revealed himself and began teaching his message. He was persecuted and driven out of his native land. The main message brought by Bahá'u'lláh was that the whole world should be united in one global society. All the barriers of race, class, religion, and nation should be broken down to unite the people of Earth. The birth and death of the Báb and the Bahá'u'lláh and the beginning of the Bahá'í faith are commemorated at festivals.

***The Bahá'ís wear a ring with a white stone** with this image. There are four Arabic letters and two stars; the stars represent the Báb and the Bahá'u'lláh.*

Life of the Báb

Siyyid 'Alí Muhammad was born in Shiraz, Persia (now Iran) in A.D. 1819. In 1844, he announced that he was the gate—the Báb in Arabic—to a new religion. The Báb said that there would soon be a messenger from God who would transform spiritual life. The authorities decided he was very dangerous and had him executed.

***The Shrine of Bahá'u'lláh is in Bahji,** just outside Akko, Israel, near where Bahá'u'lláh passed away in 1892. His death is remembered on May 29 each year.*

***The Bahá'í shrine on Mount Carmel,** northern Israel, is where the body of the Báb was placed. It is an important place of pilgrimage.*

Life of the Bahá'u'lláh

After the death of the Báb, Bahá'u'lláh (1817–1892) revealed himself as the new prophet. His name means "Glory of God." In 1863, he declared that he was the messenger foretold by the Báb. He had come to Earth to interpret God's will, which was the unity of all people. Bahá'u'lláh sent his message to kings and other heads of nations. His new religion was seen as a threat, and he was persecuted and regularly imprisoned. He was exiled from several countries, moving from Persia to Constantinople (now Istanbul) and Adrianople (now Edime) in Turkey, and Acre in Palestine. Before he died, Bahá'u'lláh appointed his son to lead the Bahá'í faith. The movement continued to grow after his death.

Celebrating the Báb and Bahá'u'lláh

Several holy days are celebrated by the Bahá'í. Nawruz is the Bahá'í New Year, which is also a spring festival. The birthday of the Báb is celebrated on October 20 with joyful community gatherings. On the birthday of Bahá'u'lláh, November 12, the Bahá'ís hold parties, exchange gifts, and send cards to friends abroad. At the 12-day Ridvan celebrations from April 21 to May 2, Bahá'ís celebrate the time in 1863 when Bahá'u'lláh stayed in a Baghdad garden, which he called the Garden of Ridvan. It was here that he proclaimed his mission as God's messenger for the world.

These Bahá'ís worship at the beautiful Bahá'í gardens *in Haifa, Israel. The Bahá'ís have a worldwide community of about 5 million followers from many nations and cultures.*

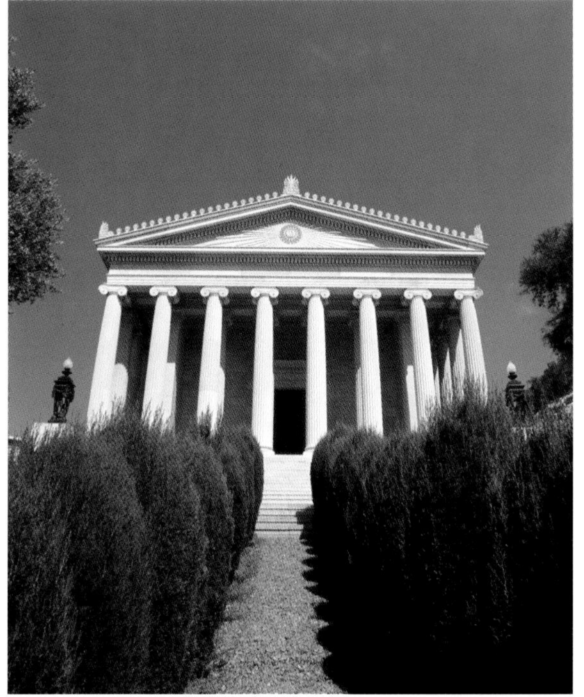

The Bahá'í International Archives Building in Israel *holds the original writings of the Báb, Bahá'u'lláh, and Ábdul-Bahá.*

PERSECUTION OF THE BAHÁ'Í

Ever since the beginning of their faith, the Bahá'ís have been persecuted, especially in Iran. They are seen as a group that has broken away from Islam, rather than members of a separate religion. In 1925, a law said that Bahá'í marriages were not valid and in 1932, Bahá'í schools in Tehran were closed down. During the 1970's, the shah's secret police organized a campaign against them. When Ayatollah Khomeini seized power in 1979, the Bahá'í religion was not recognized. To this day, powerful organizations that promote Islam harass the Bahá'ís.

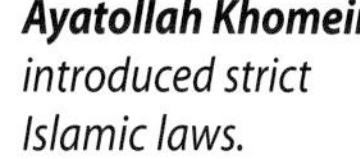

Ayatollah Khomeini *introduced strict Islamic laws.*

Scripture

The Bahá'í scriptures are formed from the writings and spoken word of the Báb, Bahá'u'lláh, and Bahá'u'lláh's son, Ábdul-Bahá. The most famous writings include *Selections from the Writings of the Báb, Tablets of Bahá'u'lláh, Kitab-i-Aqdas (Most Holy Book),* and *Kitab-i-Iqan (Book of Certitude)*. The faith is open to all who accept the teachings of Bahá'u'lláh. There is no preaching in Bahá'í temples. During services, the scriptures of many religions are recited.

This illustration is from the Bahá'í scriptures.

The four weeks before Christmas Day are known as Advent. *During Advent, one of the four candles on the Advent wreath is lit each week. Sometimes there is also a candle in the center of the wreath called the Christ candle.*

The Origins of Christmas

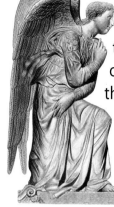

The festival of Christmas is one of the most important festivals in the Christian religion. It marks the day on which Jesus Christ, who Christians believe to have been the Son of God, was born on Earth. The story of the birth of Christ is told in the New Testament of the Bible. Over the years many other stories have been told about the birth of Christ, and these are often retold at Christmas. Since Christmas occurs in midwinter, the celebrations include features of other winter festivals that have become linked to the great Christian feast.

The winged archangel Gabriel. *The word* angel *comes from a Greek word meaning* messenger *or* one who is sent. Archangel *refers to Gabriel's high rank.*

Mary, mother of Jesus, *was frightened when Gabriel appeared, but soon accepted Gabriel's news and gave praise to God.*

The Word of Angel Gabriel

The archangel Gabriel is mentioned in the Bible as the personal messenger of God. When he came to visit a woman named Mary, Gabriel announced that Mary had found favor with God and that she was to give birth to the Son of God. He also instructed her to name the baby Jesus. Gabriel had visited Elizabeth, a relative of Mary, earlier to announce that Elizabeth would have a son. Gabriel told Zechariah, Elizabeth's husband, to name the baby John. Years later, John would announce Jesus's ministry on Earth.

An ancient painting from Greece *shows the baby Jesus in a stable with His mother, Mary, and His father, Joseph.*

The Nativity, the Birth of Christ

At the time Jesus was born, Israel was part of the Roman Empire. The emperor ordered that a census (count of the people) be taken to find out how many people lived in the empire. Every family had to go to the town of their birth to be counted, so Joseph, Mary's husband, took her to the town of Bethlehem. None of the inns had a spare room because so many people had come to Bethlehem for the census. Joseph and Mary were obliged to stay in a stable, and it was here that Jesus was born. The newborn baby was laid in a manger (trough) and wrapped in cloth to be warm and comfortable.

EUROPE

Europe is one of the smallest of the world's seven continents in area but one of the largest in population. Europe extends from the Arctic Ocean in the north to the Mediterranean Sea in the south and from the Atlantic Ocean in the west to the Ural Mountains in the east. The 47 countries of Europe include the world's largest country, Russia, as well as the world's smallest, Vatican City. Russia and Turkey lie partly in Europe and partly in Asia.

The Visit of the Shepherds

The Bible records that on the night that Jesus was born, angels visited a group of shepherds on the hills near Bethlehem to tell them that a baby had been born who would grow up to be the Savior of the world. The shepherds hurried to the stable to see Jesus and to give thanks to God.

A warm coat, shepherd's crook, *and other tools would have been used by the shepherds who visited the baby Jesus.*

MAKE A NATIVITY SCENE

- old Christmas cards
- scissors
- a shoebox
- 2 large sheets of black or dark blue construction paper
- star stickers
- glue

Fig. 1

Look through old Christmas cards for images of the traditional Nativity scene figures.

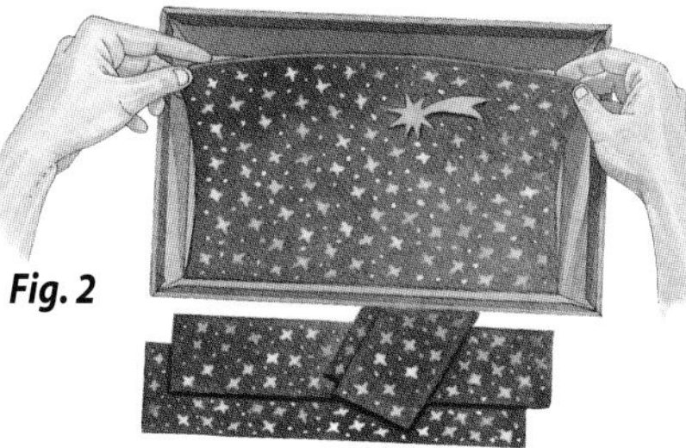

Fig. 2

Cut the figures from the cards, leaving a ½-inch flap at the bottom edge of each figure (Fig. 1). Cut pieces of black or dark blue construction paper to fit in the back and short sides of the shoebox. Decorate with star stickers to create a night sky effect. Glue the construction paper (with the sides with the stars facing out) and stick firmly to the back and sides of the shoebox (Fig. 2).

Fold the flaps beneath the Nativity figures. Glue the bottom of the flaps and stick down around the bottom of the shoebox to create your Nativity scene (Fig. 3).

Fig. 3

***The old man Simeon is shown holding the baby Jesus** in this scene of the presentation in the Temple.*

Presentation in the Temple

After the census had taken place, Mary and Joseph took Jesus to the great Temple in Jerusalem to present Him to God. At the Temple, they were met by an old man named Simeon. Because Simeon had led a holy life, he had been promised by God that he would not die until he had seen the Savior of the world. When Simeon saw the baby Jesus, he asked to hold the infant, then said, "Oh Lord, now I may die in peace for I have seen the child who is to be a glory to all people."

***The killing of the babies in Bethlehem** by soldiers sent by King Herod is known as the Massacre of the Innocents.*

***Baby Jesus escaped the massacre** when His parents fled to live in Egypt.*

The Flight into Egypt

The kingdom of Israel was ruled by King Herod on behalf of the Romans. Herod's wise men (astrologers) told him that a baby boy born in Bethlehem would grow up to be the king of Israel. Herod sent soldiers to kill all the baby boys in Bethlehem. Joseph was warned in a dream that the soldiers were coming, so he fled with Mary and the baby Jesus. They went to live in Egypt until after Herod was dead, and it was safe to return home.

A choir boy sings carols *during a Christmas church service. He wears a traditional robe.*

Caroling and Worshiping

Today, Christmastime church services take place on the four Sundays before Christmas, on Christmas Eve, and on Christmas Day itself. Festive services of music and readings from scripture also may be held in churches on other days during the season. The services are often adapted so that children play a special role in them, either singing or acting out the story of Christmas. Special hymns called "carols" are sung at these services. These carols praise God and His son Jesus Christ and often recount the stories about the birth of Jesus from the Bible.

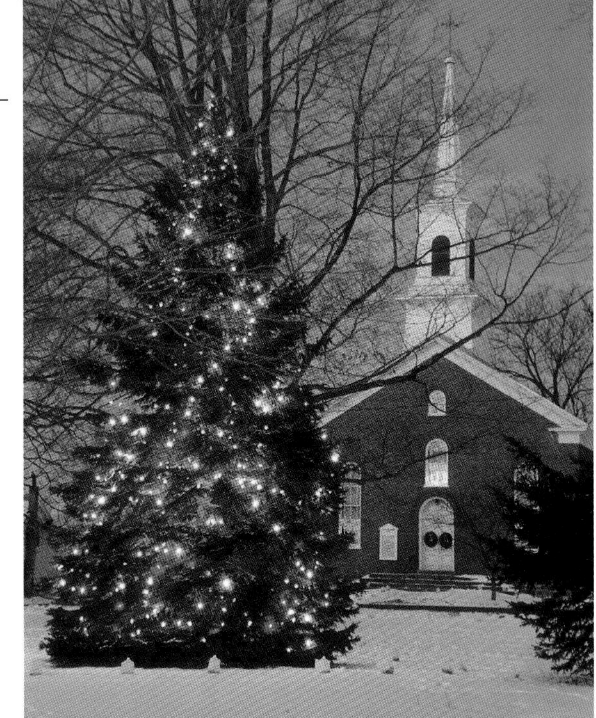

A decorated evergreen tree and wreaths on the church doors *announce the festive season to parishioners and passers-by alike.*

A large roasted turkey *dominates the Christmas table at a traditional Christmas Day meal served in the United States.*

Christmas Feasts and Sweets

A central part of Christmas celebrations is a large and luxurious meal enjoyed on Christmas Day. All the family are invited to the meal, which is usually much richer and more elegant than normal. In the past, the Christmas dinner has centered around huge cuts of roast beef or venison, but today it is usual to roast a large turkey. The dessert is usually a traditional dish, such as plum pudding in England or a panettone cake in Italy.

CHRISTIANS GIVE EACH OTHER PRESENTS AT CHRISTMAS TO IMITATE THE PRESENTS GIVEN TO JESUS WHEN HE WAS BORN. Children believe that the gifts are brought by Santa Claus, who visits on the night of Christmas Eve, December 24th. Cards are sent to share the Christmas spirit with people who will not be present on Christmas Day. The first Christmas card was created in 1843 by the Englishman John Calcott Horsley.

CHRISTMAS CAKE

- 1 ¼ cups butter, softened
- 1 ¼ cups firmly packed brown sugar
- 4 eggs
- 2 tablespoons orange marmalade
- 7 ¾ cups mixed dried fruit
- 1 ½ cups all-purpose flour
- ½ cup self-rising flour
- 2 teaspoons mixed spice
- ½ cup + 2 tablespoons sweet sherry
- ¼ cup whole almonds

Preheat the oven to 300 °F. Line the base and sides of a 7 ½-inch square cake pan with three layers of waxed paper. In a small bowl, beat the butter and sugar with an electric mixer at high speed until just blended. Beat in the eggs, one at a time, until just blended. Transfer the mixture to a large bowl. Mix in the marmalade and fruit until well mixed. Sift the flours and spice over the mixture. Add in ½ cup of sherry, mixing well. Spoon the mixture into the prepared pan. With a large rubber spatula, break any air bubbles and smooth the surface. Sprinkle the almonds over. Bake for 3 hours. Remove from the oven and brush the top with the remaining 2 tablespoons sherry. Cover the pan tightly with foil and cool completely.

Celebrating Christ

This painting shows Jesus Christ holding up a piece of bread at the Last Supper.

Jesus is shown in the shape of a cross. *The cross reminds Christians of Jesus's suffering and death on the cross and His Resurrection.*

Christians celebrate Christmas to commemorate the day on which Jesus Christ, the Son of God, is believed to have been born on Earth. Christmas, however, is only one of the many feast days on which Christians remember Christ. Holy Week, which commemorates the last days of Jesus's life on Earth, and Easter, which celebrates Jesus's Resurrection, also are important days in the Christian calendar. These feast days occur in spring. Christians also celebrate Christ in many other ways besides feast days. Sunday worship services and Bible study are only two of these.

In Remembrance of Christ

During regular Sunday church services, Catholics celebrate Mass and Protestants celebrate Holy Communion, also called the Lord's Supper. This sacrament is central to Christian worship and is done in memory of Christ. Just as Christ blessed the bread and wine, saying "this is my body" and "this is my blood" during His last meal with His disciples, the priest or minister blesses and distributes the host (a piece of bread or wafer) and wine or grape juice to the congregation. Roman Catholics believe that during this celebration the bread and wine (or juice) actually become the body and blood of Christ.

This illustration from a Byzantine Gospel shows the four evangelists, *or Gospel writers, holding their Gospels.*

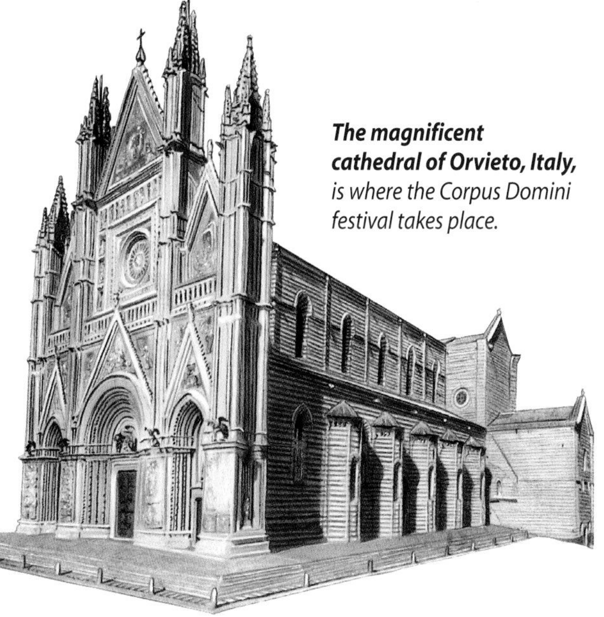

The magnificent cathedral of Orvieto, Italy, *is where the Corpus Domini festival takes place.*

Corpus Domini

In 1263, a miracle took place in Italy when the host used in the Communion service began to ooze blood onto an altar cloth. The miraculous cloth and host were preserved in the cathedral. Each year a festival called Corpus Domini (Body of God) is held in Orvieto to commemorate the miracle.

The Gospels

The Gospels of Matthew, Mark, Luke, and John are found in the New Testament of the Bible. They tell the story of the life of Jesus. The word *gospel* is an Old English word that means good news. For Christians the good news is the message of Jesus Christ. During worship services on Sundays, passages from the Gospels are read to the congregation. The words of the Gospels give worshipers moral lessons and inspiration.

Joseph Smith receives the Book of Mormon *from the angel Moroni.*

MORMONISM IN THE UNITED STATES

The Church of Jesus Christ of Latter-day Saints was founded in 1830 in the United States. Its followers, known as Mormons, believe that their founder, Joseph Smith (1805-1844), was visited by an angel called Moroni. According to Mormon beliefs, Smith translated the *Book of Mormon,* a supplement to the Bible, revealed to him by the angel. The *Book of Mormon* tells the story of how Jesus visited the Americas after his Resurrection. The book also teaches that Jesus will return to the Americas to reign over the world. Mormon headquarters are located in Salt Lake City, Utah. Mormons have a great sense of community. Most Mormons contribute a portion of their income to the church, and young men dedicate 2 years of their lives in service of the church, and young women serve 18 months.

American Indian Celebrations

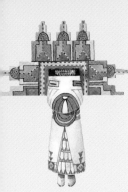

The native peoples of North America are made up of dozens of groups and nations, each with its own culture and its own set of beliefs. Many groups believed in a great sky god who was more powerful than all the other gods and spirits. This Great Spirit was thought to have created the world and all forms of life. Once the work of creation was over, the Great Spirit retired to the highest level of the sky. Although he watched over his creation, he left running Earth to lesser gods and spirits. Below the ground lived the Great Panthers and other evil spirits that brought death and suffering to humans.

This kachina doll made by Pueblo Indians *of the Southwestern States represents a god or goddess.*

This mask represents a sky god. *When the flaps are pulled shut, the mask becomes a thunderbird, a messenger of the gods. The mask was made by the Kwakiutl people.*

The Spirits of the Inuit People

The Inuit people of the Arctic did not believe in a single creator god or gods. They believed in powerful spirits that controlled all aspects of life. One of the major spirits was the Moon Spirit. This male spirit was a hunter who ruled over the animals. Since survival in the brutal arctic conditions depended on hunting animals, such as seals, walruses, and whales, the Moon Spirit was especially important.

Spirit Masks

The peoples of the Northwest lived among forests and became highly skilled woodcarvers. A central element of many religious rituals was a dance by masked men who acted out a story about the gods. In some groups, it was believed to be unlucky to tell all of a story, so only part would be acted out at one time, several rituals being needed to relate a complete tale. The Northwest Indians believed in a vast number of different gods. As well as the main gods of fire, rain, or sun, each location had its own special guardian spirit. It was essential to avoid upsetting or angering the many gods or they would bring bad luck.

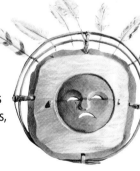

This Moon Spirit mask is from Alaska. *Today most of the Inuit have converted to Christianity and have kept traditional beliefs alive by incorporating them into Christian beliefs.*

THE AMERICAS

The continents of North America and South America make up the Western Hemisphere. North America contains Canada, Greenland, the United States, Mexico, Central America, and the Caribbean Sea islands. South America contains Argentina, Bolivia, Brazil (which occupies almost half the continent), Chile, Colombia, Ecuador, French Guiana, Guyana, Paraguay, Peru, Suriname, Uruguay, and Venezuela.

The Iroquois believed the world was created by toads, otters, and other animals *as a home for the Sky Woman after the swans could no longer support her on the waters.*

Creation Myths

The Iroquois people of the Northeast believed that the world began when the Sky Woman, daughter of the Great Spirit, became ill and fell from the sky. She was saved by two swans, who carried her on their backs. Then a toad brought up mud from the depths of the sea and spread it on the back of the Great Turtle. This mud grew to become Earth, and the Sky Woman gave birth to the first people. In the Northwest, however, the Tsimshian and other native people believed that the world was created by the Great Raven.

The Sun Dance

The most important religious ritual of the peoples who lived on the Great Plains was the Sun Dance, held in the middle of summer. A tall pole was erected on top of which was built a "nest" of twigs to symbolize the home of the Thunderbird, which could bring rain. A group of the finest warriors began to dance around this pole, blowing on whistles made from eagle bones. One or two dancers were attached to the pole by ropes tied to wooden skewers pushed through the muscles of their chest. They danced until the skewers tore free, causing excruciating pain. Warriors performed the Sun Dance to give thanks to the Great Spirit and to ask the spirit to provide for their needs.

BUFFALO SKULLS WERE PLACED ON THE GROUND DURING THE SUN DANCE to attract the attention of the Buffalo Spirit in the hope that he would ensure plenty of buffalo to hunt in the coming year.

A Native American from the Great Plains *paints a picture on a stretched buffalo hide to record an important ritual dance.*

Two warriors take part in the Sun Dance. *The dancer tied to the pole would be in great agony and might gain a vision from the Great Spirit.*

Catholicism of the Pueblo

The people of the Southwest live in villages of flat-topped houses, which are called pueblos. When the Spanish settlers arrived in the A.D. 1590's, they conquered the Pueblo groups and began converting them to Christianity. In 1680, the Pueblos began a 12-year war to throw out the Spanish and killed more than 400 Spaniards. Over the years that followed, the Pueblos adapted elements of the Christian religion to form part of their own beliefs. Each pueblo has a Christian patron saint and a church, but the people also retain belief in the old gods and perform traditional rituals and dances.

A small boy from a Pueblo settlement *has his face painted and wears a traditional headdress for a religious ceremony.*

Celebrations in Latin America

The Christian church at Guadalupe *was built on the site of an ancient temple.*

Before Christian Europeans came to the Americas, the people of Latin America followed a complex religion that included many different gods, festivals, and rituals. Many of the ancient cities were dominated by large temples dedicated to their gods. When the Europeans arrived in the Americas, many of the native peoples were forced to convert to Christianity, and their temples were destroyed to build churches. Today the majority of the people of this area are Roman Catholic. In some areas local traditions still survive alongside Christianity. Some of the biggest Christian festivals are a mix of local traditions and Christian devotion.

In Guatemala, female shamans called midwives *are highly respected for their ability to communicate with the spirits.*

Indigenous Beliefs

The Kamayura people of Brazil dress in sacred costumes and dance to ancient music to honor their gods. They believe that the brightly colored forest birds brought sunlight to Earth. In other areas, such as Guatemala, many people have preserved aspects of indigenous Mayan practices. Shamans are believed to be mediators who perform rituals to communicate with the spirit world.

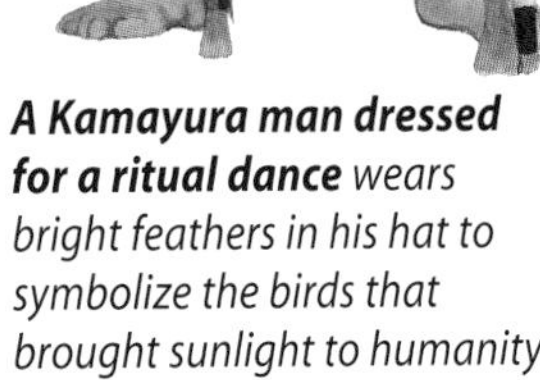

A Kamayura man dressed for a ritual dance *wears bright feathers in his hat to symbolize the birds that brought sunlight to humanity.*

A religious dance *is held in front of the Basilica of Guadalupe on December 12, the feast day of Our Lady of Guadalupe.*

Our Lady of Guadalupe

The most important sacred figure in Latin America is the Virgin Mary, celebrated as Our Lady of Guadalupe. On December 9, 1531, Juan Diego, a Mexican Indian, climbed Tepeyac Hill in what is now Mexico City. He claimed to have been met there by the Virgin Mary, who instructed Juan Diego to go to the bishop of Mexico and ask him to build a shrine on the hill. Juan did as he was told, but the bishop did not believe him. On December 12, Juan again had a vision of the Virgin, who told him to collect in his cloak the roses that were growing on the hill. Juan took the flowers to the bishop and found that a picture of the Virgin Mary had miraculously appeared on his cloak. The bishop was convinced, and a church was built on the spot where Juan Diego had his vision.

Christmas Traditions

Christmas is one of the biggest festivals in Latin America. On Christmas Eve, the children try to break the piñata. The piñata is a large earthenware vase that is brightly painted and then filled with sweets, toys, and other gifts. It is suspended by a rope either in the street or in a hall and is jerked about by an adult pulling on the rope. The children take turns being blindfolded and try to hit the piñata with a large stick. When the piñata breaks, the gifts are scattered across the floor and everyone scrambles to get a share.

A blindfolded child *tries to smash a star-shaped piñata.*

Many Rastafarians wear uncombed locks *called dreadlocks and grow beards.*

RASTAFARIANISM

Rastafarianism, founded in Jamaica during the late 1920's, is a political and religious movement of the majority black population. Early Rastafarians considered the former Ethiopian emperor, Haile Selassie (1892–1975), to have been the messiah (savior) of the black race. They believed that one day they would be free to return to their homeland in Africa, the land from which their ancestors were taken as slaves. On July 23, Rastafarians celebrate the birthday of Haile Selassie.

Manuelito

In Peru, the feast of Christmas centers around a Nativity scene made up of model farm animals, Mary, Joseph, and the baby Jesus. The figure of Jesus is in the form of a beautiful baby made of plaster and wood. When Christmas is over, most of the figures are packed away, but the Jesus figure, known as Manuelito, is put in a special vase and kept on display. On Christmas Eve, the Manuelito is taken to the local church, where the priest blesses it for use in the Christmas Nativity scene. The most expensive Manuelitos have a tiny heart of pure gold put inside them.

A Manuelito *symbolizes Christ, and one is kept in most Peruvian homes.*

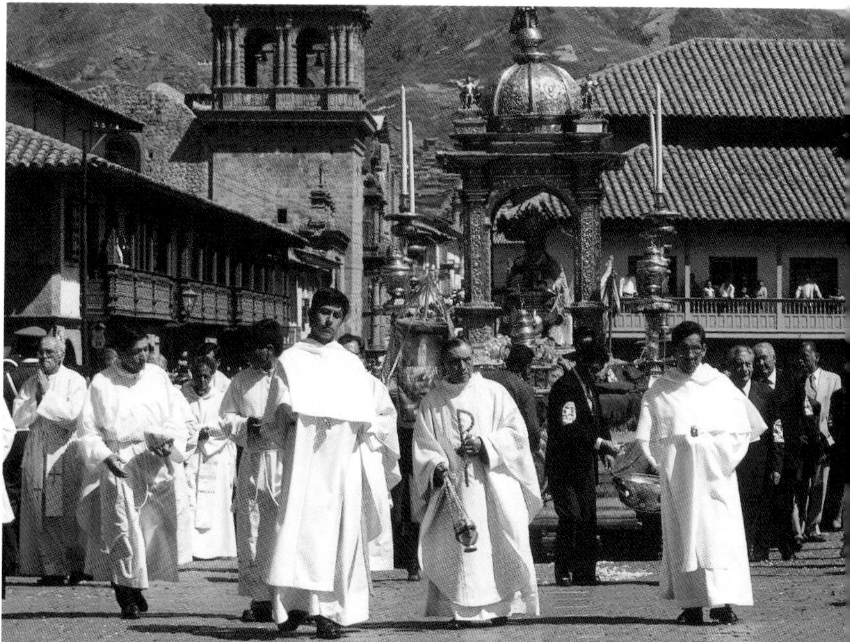

Priests lead a Corpus Christi procession *through the city of Cuzco in Peru.*

Feast of Corpus Christi

In Latin America the Christian festival of Corpus Christi is celebrated with more enthusiasm than in many other Christian countries. Corpus Christi celebrates the Body of Christ as changed in the Eucharist. It is observed on the Thursday after Trinity Sunday. (Trinity Sunday is the first Sunday after Pentecost. Pentecost is the seventh Sunday after Easter.) The Roman Catholic festival began in the A.D. 1200's. It marks the Last Supper of Jesus. Worshipers receive Communion and, in some countries, the consecrated host (bread or wafer regarded as the body of Christ) is paraded through the streets.

African Celebrations of Prophets and Gods

An illustration of the evangelist Matthew and translators from an Ethiopian gospel of the 1600's. *The spread of Christianity in Ethiopia was aided by the translation of the Gospels beginning in the 300's.*

Africa

Africa is home to dozens of religious beliefs, methods of worship, and ritualized gods. Over the centuries, Christian and Muslim beliefs have been added to this rich mix of religions. In some areas, the people have become Christian or Muslim and have abandoned their old ways. Elsewhere, the Africans have taken elements of the new religions and integrated them into the local religion, creating a vibrant combination of cultures and festivals.

Celebrating Maskal

According to legend, the Ethiopian Emperor Dawit gathered pieces of the True Cross (the cross upon which Jesus was crucified) from the Middle East when the area was conquered by the Muslims and brought them to Ethiopia. The pieces are still stored in the monastery of Gishen Mariam. On September 27, the people of Ethiopia hold the festival of Maskal to celebrate the arrival of the True Cross in their country. The largest Maskal celebration is held in the capital, Addis Ababa. A procession of priests, monks, and clergy marches to Maskal Square, where a large bonfire is lit before dancing, singing, and other festivities take place.

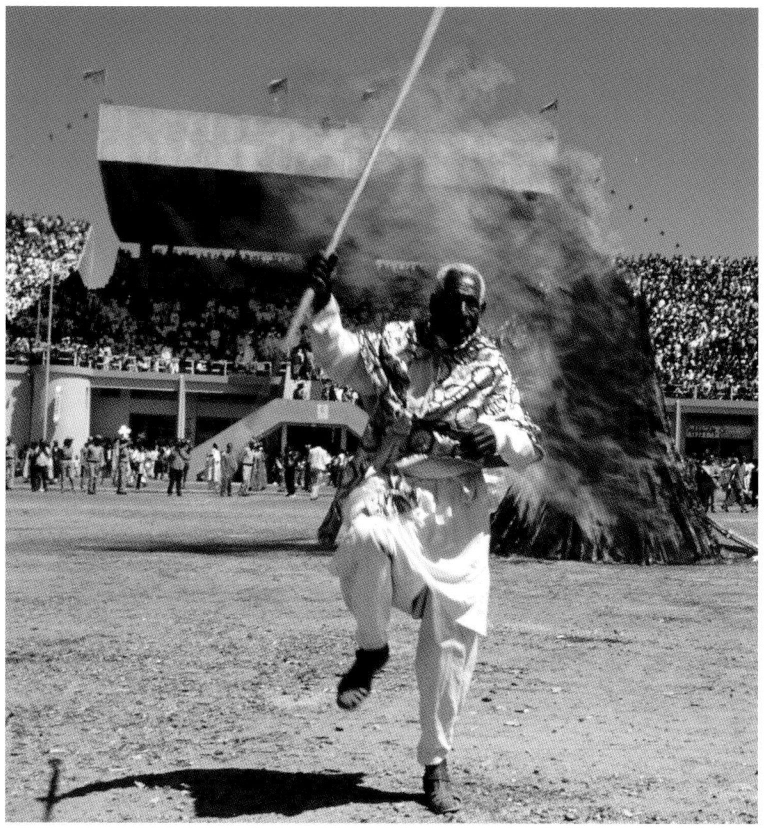

A priest dances *in front of the ritual fire as part of the celebrations of Maskal.*

AFRICA

Africa lies south of Europe and west of Asia and contains 53 independent countries. Tropical rain forests dominate western and central Africa. The world's largest desert, the Sahara, stretches across northern Africa. Africa also has the world's longest river—the Nile. Much of the continent is grassland. In the north, most of the people are Arabs. The great majority of the African population lives south of the Sahara.

VOODOO

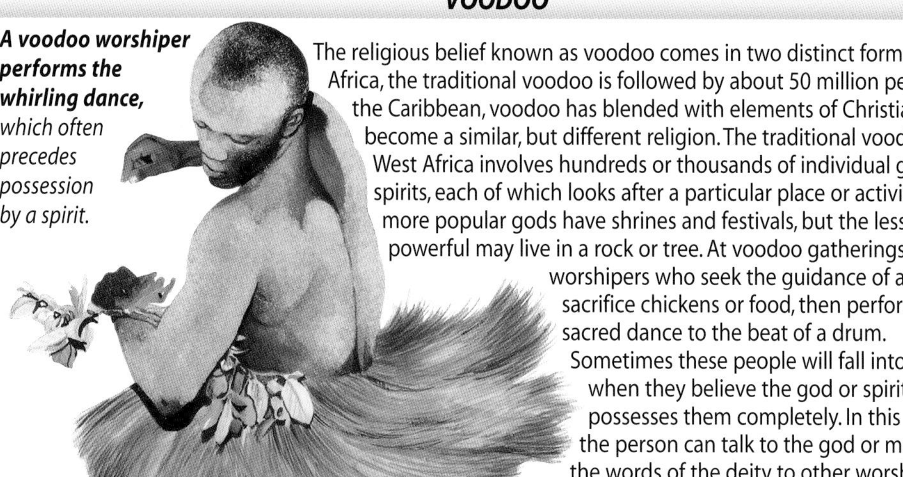

A voodoo worshiper performs the whirling dance, *which often precedes possession by a spirit.*

The religious belief known as voodoo comes in two distinct forms. In West Africa, the traditional voodoo is followed by about 50 million people. In the Caribbean, voodoo has blended with elements of Christianity to become a similar, but different religion. The traditional voodoo of West Africa involves hundreds or thousands of individual gods and spirits, each of which looks after a particular place or activity. The more popular gods have shrines and festivals, but the less powerful may live in a rock or tree. At voodoo gatherings, worshipers who seek the guidance of a god will sacrifice chickens or food, then perform a sacred dance to the beat of a drum. Sometimes these people will fall into a trance, when they believe the god or spirit possesses them completely. In this trance the person can talk to the god or may speak the words of the deity to other worshipers.

An ancient Ethiopian painting illustrates the Christmas story, *with Mary, center, holding the newborn baby Jesus.*

Ethiopian Christmas

The Christians of Ethiopia celebrate Christmas on January 7, which they call Ganna. The festival of Ganna is named after a ball game, played by knocking a hard ball with wooden sticks. The Ethiopians believe that the shepherds played a game of Ganna with their shepherd's crooks when the angel told them of the birth of Christ. It is traditional for the Ethiopians to play a game of Ganna after attending church on Christmas Day. After the game they go home for a meal of spicy chicken stew and bread.

A stilt walker *takes part in the Fetu Afahye Festival.*

Fetu Afahye Festival, Ghana

On the first Saturday of September, the people of Oguaa, on the Ghana coast, celebrate their Fetu Afahye festival. The festival is a celebration of the power and influence of the traditional kings and chiefs of the area. The rulers dress in their ceremonial costumes and are carried through the streets in chairs to a large square. There they watch a display of traditional dances to the throbbing sound of the tribal drums, followed by parades and musket practice by the warriors of the area in traditional costume.

A crowd of Ethiopians *gather after a Christmas Day church service in Lalibela to watch a game of Ganna.*

A masked dancer *wears an elaborate hat during the Fetu Afahye Festival in the West African state of Ghana.*

The ferocious war god Ku *demanded sacrifices of blood in Hawaii.*

Australasia and Oceania

Worship in Oceania and Polynesia

The nations of Oceania and Polynesia enjoy a wide variety of festivals traditional to the different peoples who live there. The native peoples worshiped a number of gods and goddesses, all with their own festivals and rituals. The Europeans who have come to the area brought with them their own festivals, but because the seasons in the Southern Hemisphere are the opposite of those in Europe, there can be some confusion. Christmas, for instance, happens in summer, not in winter.

The Polynesian hero Maui *pulls a giant fish from the ocean. The fish became New Zealand.*

Maui—God of a Thousand Tricks

One of the most popular gods of Polynesia was Maui, the trickster god. Maui was born a weak baby, but he was cared for by the gods of the sea and grew to be an intelligent and powerful hero. One story tells how Maui was fishing in the ocean when he caught a massive fish with a magic fish hook. The huge fish became New Zealand. New Zealand is only one of the islands that is said to be Maui's fish; other islands are also reputed to have been fished up by Maui.

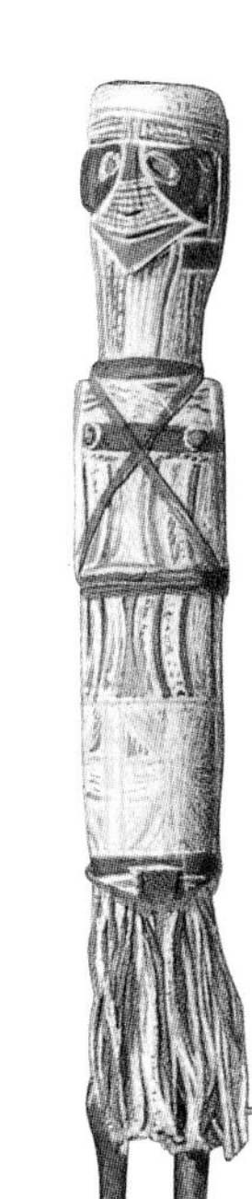

The ancestral being Djanggawul and his two sisters *are depicted in these wooden figures.*

Aborigine Primal Beings

According to Aborigine myth, ancestors, or primal beings, created the landscape and society. Djanggawul and his two sisters are among them. They arrived in the northern lands of Australia from the underworld. They gave Australia its landscape and vegetation.

AUSTRALASIA AND OCEANIA

Australasia and Oceania lie east of Asia and west of the Americas. Australasia refers to the continent of Australia, plus New Guinea, New Zealand, and other nearby islands. New Guinea and New Zealand are also considered as part of the Pacific Islands, or Oceania. Oceania is a name given to a group of many thousands of islands scattered across the Pacific Ocean. New Guinea is the largest island in the group. It contains Papua, which is a part of Indonesia, and the independent country of Papua New Guinea. Islands near the mainland of Asia (Indonesia, Japan, the Philippines) are part of Asia. Islands near North and South America (the Aleutians, the Galapagos) are grouped with those continents.

ANCESTOR WORSHIP

Many of the native peoples of Oceania believe that the spirits of their ancestors are able to watch over them. The ancestors can bring good or bad luck, depending on whether or not they agree with what the people are doing. It is therefore important to explain to the ancestors what is being done and to offer them gifts to win their favor. When boys grow up, they often take part in a ceremony to mark the fact that they have become men. In New Guinea, men wearing masks representing the ancestors dance through the villages to welcome the boys to the adult world of the tribe.

This mask of a male ancestor spirit *is used in a dance in New Guinea.*

Murukan Worship in Melbourne

One of the peoples who settled in Oceania are the Tamils of southern India, who have established communities in many areas. One of the largest Tamil centers is in Melbourne, where they have built several temples. Among the most popular of the Hindu gods brought to Australia by the Tamils is Murukan, a god of youth and strength who is believed to have fought the demons and driven them from Earth. The birthday of Murukan is celebrated in summer with sacred fires.

Tamils celebrate the birthday of the hero god Murukan, right, *with sacred fires, onto which are thrown incense and food.*

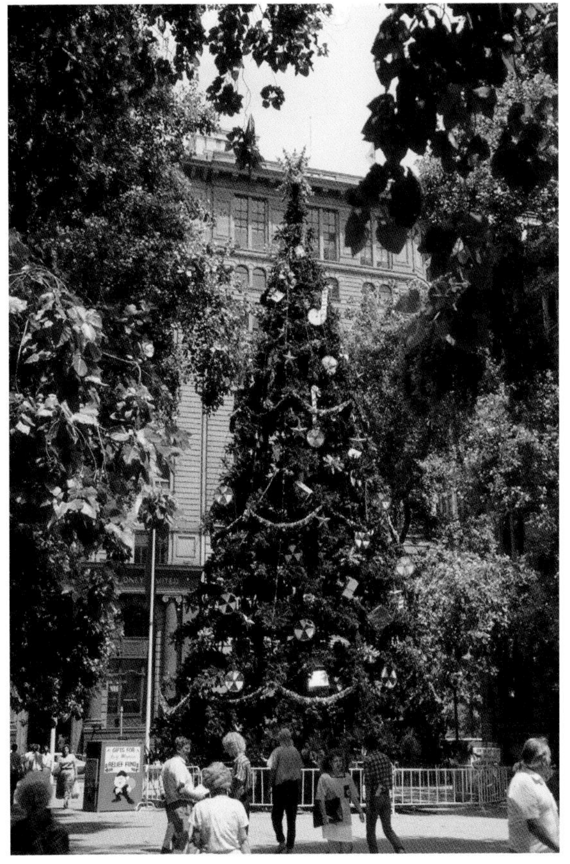

Christmas Celebrations in Summer

The settlers who came to Oceania and Polynesia before the 1950's came mainly from northern Europe. One of the most important festivals these people brought with them was Christmas. In northern Europe, Christmas occurs in midwinter when the weather is cold and snow often covers the ground. But in the South Pacific, Christmas falls in midsummer when the weather is hot. The earliest European settlers continued with the traditions and festivals they had brought from home. Gradually, the people in Oceania and Polynesia began to abandon those traditions that did not fit with the hot weather. Aside from the religious services, Christmas celebrations for Australia and New Zealand's Protestant majority may be a day on the beach. Seafood meals with barbecued crayfish are becoming a tradition.

***A summertime Christmas tree decorates a street in Australia,* left.**

BECAUSE THE CHRISTMAS WEATHER IN AUSTRALIA IS SO WARM AND SUNNY, people have begun to celebrate the festival with outdoor activities. In Perth, Western Australia, a huge Christmas pageant is held each year. The highlight is a parade of floats, people wearing fancy costumes, and musicians. Another popular Christmas activity in the South Pacific is yachting. The most important event is the Sydney to Hobart Yacht Race, which starts on December 26 each year and ends three days later.

The Tiwi Islands

On the Tiwi Islands, just off Australia's northern coast, indigenous beliefs have mixed with Christian beliefs. Since the founding of the Catholic mission in 1911, the people of these islands have kept their own distinct cultural identity while embracing Christian beliefs. Every year, many of the native Tiwi ceremonies, accompanied by song and dance, are still held to celebrate life by people of the Tiwi Islands.

The interior of a Catholic church on Melville Island *is decorated with traditional Tiwi designs.*

Glossary

Abstain To give up doing something; to do without something.

Abundance A quantity that is more than enough, or a great supply.

Agriculture The science, art, or occupation of cultivating the soil to make crops grow and of raising farm animals.

Ancestor A family member from a preceding generation to whom you are directly related, for example, a grandfather or great-grandfather.

Blessing Divine favor or protection. An approval or wish for happiness.

Caste One of the social classes into which Hindus are divided.

Ceremony The celebration of an important event with an act or series of acts that follow a set of instructions established by a religion, culture, or country.

Chant To sing in one tone or to repeat a prayer many times. A song or hymn used in religious ritual.

Commemorate To honor the memory of a special historical or religious event with a celebration or ceremony.

Convert To change religion or religious beliefs. To become something else.

Crop A large number of plants of any given kind that are grown for human use.

Culture A way of life. Every human society has a culture that includes its arts, beliefs, customs, institutions, inventions, language, technology, and values.

Deity A god or goddess.

Devotion Earnestness in religion; religious worship or observance; act of devoting to a sacred use or purpose.

Divine Sacred, being related to a god or goddess.

Dwelling A building used as a home or shelter.

Enlightenment The act of receiving spiritual or intellectual insight or information.

Fast To choose to go without eating for a time, often for religious reasons.

Fertility The ability to produce and reproduce living things. Land is fertile when many crops can grow there.

Fortune Happiness or good luck that happens in a person's life.

Guru In Sikhism, one of 10 early leaders of religious faith. In Hinduism, a spiritual teacher.

Harvest The reaping and gathering of grain and other food crops.

Ignorance The state of not knowing; lack of knowledge.

Immortal Living forever; never dying.

Indigenous people The original people living in a country or area before other people settled there, and their descendants.

Meditate To think privately or to focus one's mind on serious or religious thoughts.

Merge To be absorbed into or to combine with something.

Monastery A place where a community of religious people, such as monks, live.

Mosque A place of worship and prayer for the followers of Islam.

Muslim A person who follows the religion of Islam.

Persecution The punishment and harassment of a person or a group of people because of their beliefs and principles, such as their religion, or because of their race or gender, or other personal characteristics.

Pilgrimage A journey taken to visit a holy place.

Possess To own. To control or influence.

Precept A rule or law of behavior.

Procession A parade held for a religious ceremony or ritual.

Prophet A person who has been inspired by God and communicates God's will or interprets God's message to the people.

Prosperous Successful; thriving; doing well; fortunate.

Recite To say something, such as a prayer or verse, to an audience or in a group of people.

Reflection The act of careful and serious thinking.

Relic An object that has remained from the past. A sacred object that once belonged to a saint or holy person, kept as a sacred memorial.

Resurrection The act of returning to life after death. On Easter, Christians celebrate Jesus's Resurrection.

Reverence A feeling of deep respect or high regard.

Ritual A set of repeated actions done in a precise way, usually with a solemn meaning or significance.

Sacred Holy or precious.

Sacrifice The killing of an animal, which is offered to a god or gods as part of worship.

Saint A holy person who becomes a recognized religious hero by displaying a virtue or virtues valued by his or her religion. A patron saint is a holy person believed to protect the interests of a country, place, group, trade, profession, or activity.

Sanctuary A sacred place or a place where sacred objects are stored.

Shaman A priest or doctor who uses magic to protect people and to cure the sick.

Shrine A small chapel, altar, or sacred place of worship.

Solemn Serious; done with ceremony; connected with religion; sacred.

Spirit A good or bad supernatural being or force.

Supernatural Not of this world; beyond nature.

Symbolize To stand for or represent.

Torah Hebrew name for the first five books of the Bible.

Tradition The beliefs, opinions, customs, and stories passed from generation to generation by word of mouth or by practice.

Trance A state somewhat like a deep sleep; high emotion.

Venerate To honor or to pay deep respect.

Widow A woman whose husband is dead and who has not married again. A widower is a man whose wife is dead and who has not married again.

Wisdom The ability to judge what is right or true. Wisdom often develops with age and life experience.

Index